The Pain of Separation

The Pain of Separation

The Shlokas of Sheik Farid
From the Guru Granth Sahib

A Commentary By
AJAIB SINGH

Sant Bani Ashram, Sanbornton, New Hampshire 2020

Our greatest thanks to
Sant Ajaib Singh Ji who helped us at every step.

The original series of talks were given by Sant Ajaib Singh
in Punjabi and later translated by Raj Kumar Bagga.
Initial translation edited from the point of view of English language
by Michael Mayo-Smith and Richard Shannon.
Formatting by Jerry-Jo Idarius at Creation-Designs
and Amy Kaufman. Proof reading by Megan Farkas,
Roberta Wiggins, Cab Vinton, and Kent Bicknell.

We are very grateful to Raj Kumar Bagga
without whose help this book would not exist
and to Russell Perkins for his advice and encouragement.

ISBN: 978-0-89142-010-1 (paperback)
Library of Congress Control Number: 2020941562
Sant Bani Ashram, Inc., 2020

TABLE OF CONTENTS

Foreward vii
Preface xi

Chapter 1   On the Soul's Wedding Day 3
Chapter 2   The Disease of Yearning 23
Chapter 3   The Pain of Separation 45
Chapter 4   God Will Call for Your Account 67
Chapter 5   The Days Are Passing 85
Chapter 6   I Hope to See My Lord 101
Chapter 7   Let Patience Become Your Nature 131
Chapter 8   The Alms of Devotion and Love 155

Glossary 169

FOREWARD

SANT AJAIB SINGH AND SANT MAT

The author of this book, Sant Ajaib Singh Ji (1926-1997) of Village 16 PS, Rajasthan, India, was a perfect disciple of the great Master Kirpal Singh Ji Maharaj (1894-1974) of Delhi, India, the inheritor of his mantle, and a powerful and loving exponent of his teaching. This teaching, the ancient esoteric tradition found at the core of all revealed religions and scriptures, is known in modern India as *Sant Mat,* or the Path of the Masters. It is based on the fact that God is love and thus that love is the core of the universe. It is not a belief system but an actual path, or highway, that leads from the individual soul into the heart of God by way of his Word or Name *(Naam),* the Word or Name that created the universe, proceeds from him and leads back to him. The Masters of this path teach that the Word or Name of God is present within all of us by virtue of our existence and can, with the grace of God, be seen, heard and felt by each individual. Under the guidance of the Master we can follow this Word or Name (often referred to by the Masters as the "Sound Current") back to its source and thus achieve liberation from the cycle of births and deaths and the limitations of the human condition.[1]

As said above, this teaching is universal and found within all religious traditions. It was first taught apart from any particular religion by Kabir (1398-1518), a Muslim Saint of north India who taught that there was no essential difference between Islam and Hinduism (or any other religion) and who gave of his grace freely to all seekers, regardless of religion, caste or ethnic origin. Kabir in turn influenced many others and founded several

---

[1] For a beautiful and comprehensive description of Sant Mat the reader is referred to the books of Kirpal Singh, including *The Crown of Life: A Study in Yoga, Godman, Naam or Word, Spirituality: What It Is,* and others.

lines of Masters, including the ten Gurus of the Sikhs, which continue down to the present day. In modern times there has been a succession of great Masters, including Swami Ji Maharaj of Agra (1818-1878), Baba Jaimal Singh (1838-1903) and Baba Sawan Singh (1858-1948) of Beas, and the Masters Kirpal and Ajaib, all of whom taught the same path and gave out the same love and grace.[2] Ajaib Singh, the author of this book, sat at the feet of both Sawan and Kirpal and was an initiate of the latter. He refers to both of them many times in the course of the book.

THIS BOOK

During his lifetime, Sant Ajaib Singh supervised the translation of Kabir's epic poem, published as *The Ocean of Love: the Anurag Sagar of Kabir*. Three additional books, consisting of his commentary on important sections of the Guru Granth Sahib, the central religious scripture of Sikhism, were also published. These were: *The Jewel of Happiness: the Sukhmani of Guru Arjan*, *The Two Ways: the Gauri Vars of Guru Ram Das*, and *In the Palace of Love: the Asa di Vars of Guru Nanak*.

During his last visit to America, he came to Sant Bani Ashram in Sanbornton, NH. On July 27, 1996, he met with the Ashram's Board of Directors and concluded his remarks to them with the following: "I am very happy to see the book put together by Darryl Rubin [*The Ambrosial Hour*]. It is very good. I am sure that the *sangat* (congregation) will benefit from it. And there are other books also in the pipeline, like the *satsangs*[3] where I have commented upon Kabir Sahib's hymns and Bhai Gurdas and

---

[2] Biographical information about these Masters can be found in the following books: Kabir, *The Ocean of Love: The Anurag Sagar of Kabir*, pp xvii-xxvi; Jon Engle, *Servants of God: The Lives of the Ten Sikh Gurus;* Kirpal Singh, *Baba Jaimal Singh: His Life and Teachings* and (about Sawan Singh) *The Way of the Saints*, pp 1-40; Bhadra Sena, *The Beloved Master: Some Glimpses of the Life of Sant Kirpal Singh Ji Maharaj;* and Michael Mayo-Smith, editor, *In Search of the Gracious One: An Account in His Own Words of the Spiritual Search and Discipleship of Ajaib Singh*.

[3] A discourse given by a Saint or Master on the subject of spirituality. Also refers to the congregation where seekers gather to hear the teachings of the Saints.

Foreward

Farid Sahib, and all that. And when those books will be published, I am sure that the dear ones in the sangat will benefit from that. I know it is very hard work, it is not an easy work, to put a book together. It takes a lot to compile a book. But Guru Nanak Sahib said that we can do good for others only if we sacrifice on our part."

In addition to the three books he mentioned in his remarks, with regard to Sant Ji's reference to "and all that," at various times he also referred specifically to the publication of books of commentary on hymns by women Saints, notably Sahajo Bai,[4] and on the hymns of the Sarang Ki Var of the Guru Granth Sahib.[5] The first of these five books was published in 2010 as *The Rescue: The Vars of Bhai Gurdas*. This book, commenting on the verses of Farid, is the second in this series.

There is a reason why great spiritual Masters take the trouble to write books. Their purpose, their reason for being, is to take children of God, all of us, back to our Real Home as quickly and easily as possible. The more we understand about the Masters and the difference between illusion and reality, about the tremendous importance of human unity and the fact that "God resides in every heart," the more real the Masters' teachings are for us. As this understanding grows, the easier it is for the Master to do what he was born to do and the easier it is for us to allow him to do it. We all want to know, to understand; while it is true that knowledge and understanding come only after going within and seeing for ourselves what the Master is talking about, still we can understand a very great deal by studying and digesting the words he has provided for us. The wisdom, compassion, and

---

[4] In the satsang of 10/10/1992 on a hymn of Sahajo Bai, Sant Ji said, "Just like I commented earlier on the Gauri Var and the other *banis* (verses) from Guru Granth Sahib, which were later formed into a book and people were benefitting a lot by reading those books, in the same way the satsang which I will be commenting on Sahajo Bai's bani will be available in the form of a book later."

[5] In the satsang of 12/24/1988 Sant Ji said, "A hymn of Rag Sarang is presented to you. Rag Sarang is a section or a part of the Guru Granth Sahib. Earlier also I had commented on, I had given about six or seven talks from this same Var so that these talks may also be made available to the dear ones in the form of the book, like the book *The Two Ways* is based on talks on Rag Gauri."

The Pain of Separation

grace that Sant Ji showed in the writing of these last books can benefit us all, if we take advantage of it.

RUSSELL PERKINS
Sebastopol, California
December 2019

PREFACE

LIFE OF SHEIK FARID

Sheik Farid was born around 1173 in the village of Kothiwal in the Punjab section of what is now Pakistan, in the general vicinity of the city of Lahore. His birth name was Farid ud-din Masud.[1] His great-grandfather was the son of the emperor of Kabul and was killed in the Mongol invasions of Afghanistan. His grandfather, Shaik Sahib, was part of an emigration of educated political and religious families out of Afghanistan to India, seeking to avoid the violence and war occurring in that country but also to contribute to the establishment of Islam in India. Shaik Sahib eventually settled in Kothiwal, where he established a well-known private college for religious instruction. Farid's father was a *kazi* (Islamic jurist) and a highly educated and respected member of the community. He married a local Punjabi girl, Mariam, daughter of a local *sheik*.[2] Farid's mother was a deeply spiritual person and a major influence on Farid, inspiring him to do the devotion of the Lord.

The following story about Farid and his mother was a favorite of Sant Ajaib Singh, and frequently told in his children's satsangs.

> I have often told the story of a Sufi Saint, Sheik Farid, how in his childhood he was inspired by his mother to do the devotion of the Lord. His mother used to go very high within in her meditation, and she wanted to make the life of Sheik Farid. One day,

---

[1] Farid is a common Muslim name. Sheik Farid was a contemporary of Farid ud-din Attar, another well-known figure in Islamic mysticism, who lived in Persia and was a famous poet, author of *Conference of the Birds*.

[2] An official in a Muslim religious organization or order; also used as a title added to the names of Muslim holy men out of respect by their followers.

The Pain of Separation

she told Farid that he should do the devotion of the Lord. Farid at once said, "Well Mother, why should I do the devotion of the Lord? Is God going to give me any sugar or sweets?" His mother said, "Yes, my son, God will not only give you sugar and sweets, but he will also give you all the riches, all the things, if you do his devotion." She gave him a prayer mat to sit on, and she told him to sit for meditation. She put some sugar candy under his prayer mat so that he would be convinced that God really gives sugar when we do his devotion. After a few minutes, his mother told him, "Okay my dear son, open your eyes and see what God has given to you. Since you are doing his devotion, he has given sugar to you." Sheik Farid became very happy and he ate that sugar.

This went on for some days, and one day his mother wanted to see whether he was really interested in meditation or she was just imposing it on him. That day she did not make him sit for meditation; she told him that he should go and do something else. But Sheik Farid was not interested. He said, "Mother, I should meditate now, I should sit, because God is going to give me sugar, and I don't want God to have to wait for me."

When Sheik Farid's mother, who used to go very deep in the within, saw that he was interested in doing meditation, she gave her attention to Sheik Farid and started pulling his soul up. Gradually, when he tasted the elixir of Naam, which was the sweetest of all, he forgot the taste of sugar and all the other sweet things. Later he wrote,

O Farid, sugar candy, jaggery,[3] *honey, and buffalo milk,*
All these things are sweet. But none is equal to God's sweetness.[4]

---

[3] An unrefined form of sugar derived from sugar cane.

[4] From a children's talk on 4/28/1985 in Australia, published in *Sant Bani Magazine* April 1999, and a question-and-answer session on 12/1/1981 at Sant Bani Ashram, 16 PS, Rajasthan, India, published in *Sant Bani Magazine* January 1999.

Preface

Farid received extensive education from an early age, first at Kothiwal and then at the nearby city of Multan. When he was sixteen years old, he went on pilgrimage to Mecca with his parents. In the following years he travelled widely across the Islamic world, including Afghanistan, Baghdad, Jerusalem, Syria, Iran, Mecca and Medina, meeting many great Sufi teachers and saints.

For a period of time, Farid wandered in the forests and jungles, seeking solitude for his spiritual practices. He also practiced austerities in hopes of gaining spiritual benefit. Sant Ji comments, "The life of Sheik Farid is very similar to my own life as far as performing the austerities and things like that are concerned. I would say that he performed more austerities, that he renounced a lot more than I did."[5]

Many tales relate his performance of the *Chilla-e-Maakoos* austerity, hanging himself upside down in a well and doing meditation. In some tales he did this austerity for forty days, in others he performed it over a period of twelve years.

He was also known for his efforts to minimize his food, another similarity of his life with that of Sant Ajaib Singh.[6] Sant Ji commented on this practice in a question-and-answer session with disciples. "Baba Farid performed many practices to realize God. Once he made a structure like a chapati out of wood, and he tied that to his stomach. He did that only to help his efforts to fast. If anybody asked him, 'Do you want to eat some food?' he would say, 'No, I have already eaten, and I am full, and you see

---

[5] See Chapter 8.

[6] *In Search of the Gracious One,* p 118. Sant Ji refers to Farid when describing his own efforts to reduce his food intake. "It is very difficult to reduce the amount of food that you eat. Those who have done it know how difficult it is. Sufi Saint Farid Sahib has written, 'O Farid, hunger is worse than death. One eats at night, but the next morning again one feels hungry and feels like eating.' So, Baba Bishan Das first made me reduce my intake of food. After that he made me eat only vegetables and then he kept me on a very, very simple diet. When hunger started bothering me, many times I would cry out and I would become perturbed. I would cry out and I would say, 'Baba Ji, I feel like I am going to die.' He would say, 'No, you are not going to lose anything, you are not going to die. In fact, now you are going to live.'"

The Pain of Separation

whatever was left over I have tied that to my stomach so that I can eat next time.' Whenever he was getting much pain from hunger he would go to the trees and just break off and eat some leaves of the tree."[7]

At some point, Farid ended his wandering in the forest and his strict austerities. He developed a relationship with his spiritual Master who, by all accounts, was the Sufi Saint Qutbuddin Bakhtiar Kaki. Exactly when he met his Master cannot be determined from the historical record. Qutbuddin Bakhtiar Kaki was a disciple of the famous Sufi Master Khwaja Moinuddin Chisti whom both Sawan and Kirpal have mentioned and quoted from in their books. When Outbuddin Bakhtiar Kaki passed away, he passed the spiritual mantle to Sheik Farid. Farid came to Delhi briefly but then settled in what is now Pakpattan, in Pakistan, Punjab about forty miles west of the Indian city of Sri Ganganagar, quite close to the area where Sant Ji's ashrams were located.

Sheik Farid became widely known as Farid Ganjshakar, the "Treasury of Sugar (Sweetness)." In Pakpattan he lived a householder's life, married and with a family, but continued a life of great simplicity and devotion. He made the city a major center of Sufi thought. People from all over India and the Middle East would come to see him. It is said he used his native language, the Punjabi spoken by common people, even though he was highly learned and educated in Arabic, Persian and other languages. He wrote his verses in Punjabi which were intended to be recited or sung. They greatly influenced the local population, particularly the women who used to sing these simple verses while doing their daily chores. He is considered the father of Punjabi poetry and literature and is recognized as being the first to use the local languages of India as the language for religious writings.

As Sant Ji has noted, "He became a perfect Sufi Saint and in the area of Kasur and Bhagwatan he opened colleges, and he gave good education

---

[7] From a question-and-answer session on 8/22/1977 at Sant Bani Ashram, Sanbornton, NH, published in *Sant Bani Magazine* December 1991.

Preface

and good teachings to so many people. He made many peoples' lives; he liberated many souls; he made many Saints."[8]

Farid died in 1266. His spiritual successor was the famous Sufi Saint Nizamuddin Auliya. The stories of the love between Nizamuddin Auliya and his most beloved disciple, Amir Khusro, are well known within the Sant Mat tradition. In addition, there was a long line of religious leaders who continued Farid's work in Pakpattan.

SHEIK FARID AND THE GURU GRANTH SAHIB

Returning from his long journey to the East around 1512 AD, Guru Nanak, the first of the Sikh Gurus, stopped in Pakpattan. There he met with Sheik Ibrahim, then the living representative of the line of sheiks carrying on the work of Farid at Pakpattan. Sheik Ibrahim was a well-known religious leader, also known as Sheik Brahm, Sheik Baram, or Sheik Farid Sani (Farid the Second). As related by Kirpal Singh in his life sketch of Guru Nanak, on seeing Nanak, Sheik Ibrahim greeted him with the words, *"Allah Nu"* or "Thou are Allah." Nanak replied, "Allah is the only aim of my life. O Farid, Allah is the very essence of my being."[9] The two went on to have extensive discussions on spiritual matters; indeed, the first eight chapters of Ajaib Singh's book *In the Palace of Love: Comments on the Asa di Vars of Guru Nanak* reflect Guru Nanak's responses to Sheik Ibrahim's questions and the discussions between the two. Ajaib Singh noted that Sheik Ibrahim "asked many questions of Guru Nanak and Guru Nanak answered them all. He told him about the importance of having a living Master and about the living Master's power and what he is able to do."

It is widely believed that Sheik Ibrahim introduced Nanak to the writings of Sheik Farid. When Guru Arjan compiled the Guru Granth Sahib, a task completed in 1604, he included writings of Farid. Two *shabds* (hymns) of Farid are included in the Rag Asa section (Guru Granth Sahib, p 488)

---

[8] From a children's talk on 4/28/1985 in Australia, published in *Sant Bani Magazine* April 1999.
[9] *Jap Ji; The Message of Guru Nanak*, Kirpal Singh, p 135.

The Pain of Separation

and two shabds in the Rag Suhi section (Guru Granth Sahib, p 794). In addition, he included a segment attributed to Farid in the Rag Jaijaiwanti section (Guru Granth Sahib, pp 1377-84) with a total of one hundred and thirty verses or *shlokas* (hymns).

It was Guru Arjan's practice to sometimes include verses written by one of the first five Gurus in sections primarily authored by another individual. These additions expand, elaborate or comment on the verses of the primary author. The section containing the shlokas of Farid includes verses written by Guru Arjan and by Guru Amar Das. In the Guru Granth Sahib, Guru Arjan identified these verses by attributing them to himself or Guru Amar Das. In the text of this book the reader will see these verses preceded by a comment noting this. There are also a small number of verses which many scholars believe were written by Guru Nanak, as the verses are written as being spoken by Nanak ("O Nanak"), but are not attributed to another of the Sikh Gurus. In his commentary, Ajaib Singh also speaks to some verses as written by Guru Nanak. However, the editors chose to stay within the text of the Guru Granth Sahib and only add explicit attribution for those verses where such attribution was included by Guru Arjan.

In this book, the first seven chapters are comments on the section from Rag Jaijaiwanti. The eighth chapter is a commentary on the first shabd included in Rag Asa. The second shabd from Rag Asa and the two shabds from Rag Suhi are added to the end of this chapter, as there was no additional satsangs commenting on these verses. The following list provides the date and place of the satsang upon which the chapter is based, and the specific shlokas commented upon.

Chapter 1, "On the Soul's Wedding Day," based on satsang of January 9, 1987, Mumbai, on Rag Jaijaiwanti shlokas 1-4, Guru Granth Sahib, pp 1377-78

Chapter 2, "The Disease of Yearning," based on satsang of January 10, 1987, Mumbai, on Rag Jaijaiwanti shlokas 5-18, Guru Granth Sahib, p 1378

Chapter 3, "The Pain of Separation," based on satsang of January 11, 1987, Mumbai, on Rag Jaijaiwanti shlokas 19-36, Guru Granth Sahib, pp 1378-79

Preface

Chapter 4, "God Will Call for Your Account," based on satsang of January 12, 1987, Mumbai, on Rag Jaijaiwanti shlokas 37-50, Guru Granth Sahib, pp 1379-80

Chapter 5, "Think of That Place Where You Have to Go," based on satsang of January 13, 1987, Mumbai, on Rag Jaijaiwanti shlokas 51-75, Guru Granth Sahib, pp 1380-81

Chapter 6, "I Hope to See My Lord," based on satsang of February 8, 1987, Village 84 RB, Rajasthan, on Rag Jaijaiwanti shlokas 76-104, Guru Granth Sahib, pp 1381-83

Chapter 7, "Let Patience Become Your Nature," based on satsang of February 12, 1987, Sant Bani Ashram, Village 16 PS, Rajasthan, on Rag Jaijaiwanti shlokas 105-130, Guru Granth Sahib, pp 1383-84

Chapter 8, "The Alms of Devotion and Love," based on satsang of March 31, 1987, Sant Bani Ashram, Village 16 PS, Rajasthan, on Rag Asa shabd 1 Guru Granth Sahib, p 488, with translation of the second shabd of Rag Asa and of Rag Suhi shabds 1-2, Guru Granth Sahib, p 794 added at the end of the satsang.

MICHAEL MAYO-SMITH
Franklin, New Hampshire
December 2019

The Pain of Separation

Chapter 1

On the Soul's Wedding Day

This world has never been without the presence of Saints and Mahatmas. God Almighty has always come into this world to give his own message to the people. Sometimes he was called Guru Nanak, sometimes he was called Kabir, and the name of that same great power was once Sawan. Only those fortunate souls who have good faith take advantage of the coming of such Mahatmas into this world. We worldly people just waste all our time thinking and we do not get any benefit from them. We call ourselves true followers of the Mahatmas but we give up the path of Shabd Naam and try to realize God just by doing rites and rituals and good deeds. We try to confine the sacred teachings from the hearts of Mahatmas to a certain area and we give the form of religion to those teachings, but by doing this we confine those teachings to only a few people and we try to show that we are the only real followers of those Mahatmas. But dear ones, that is not true. Only he is a true follower of the Master who follows the Master's orders and who practices all the teachings of the Master himself.

The religious scriptures written by the Masters are like milestones to make our journey easier. Mahatmas worked very hard. They stayed up many nights, suffered hunger and thirst, and they worked very hard in order to manifest God Almighty within themselves. Rising above their physical bodies, they connected themselves with Almighty Lord. Whatever they

The Pain of Separation

saw, whatever they had to face, and whatever they did, they wrote down in the holy books for our guidance.

Nowhere in the writings of perfect Mahatmas will you find that they have written that God is somewhere outside. If they had found God Almighty somewhere outside, they would have written that. But since they found him only within themselves, they have written in their holy books that God can only be found within. If you read any holy book which rises above religious beliefs, you will find it written there that God cannot be found anywhere outside. He is neither on top of the mountains, nor in the depth of the oceans. No matter how beautiful or how good a temple you make for him, he will not come and live there, because God Almighty himself has made the temple, this human body, in which he resides. If you enter this temple, if you purify this house, only then will you meet Almighty God. All ten of the great Sikh Gurus, from Guru Nanak to Guru Gobind Singh, worked very hard and they preached the path of Surat Shabd. The goal of Surat Shabd Yoga is the union of the *surat*, our attention, with the Shabd, Almighty Lord. Our soul is within us and God Almighty, the Shabd, is also within us. Now we are not connected and that is why we have not realized him.

After people forgot the teachings of Guru Nanak and Kabir, after they forgot the path of Surat Shabd, in order to make those teachings fresh for people, God Almighty came in the body of Baba Sawan Singh. No Mahatma tells us anything new. They tell us that the path of God is not created by any human being. It is created by God himself. No one can increase that path; no one can decrease that path; no one can do any alteration to it. That path of God is as old as God himself. Saints and Mahatmas do not come into this world to attach us to any particular community or religion. They neither form any new religious community nor do they break any of the existing ones. They tell us, "Dear ones, do the meditation of Surat Shabd while living in your religions and communities and, while maintaining your religious beliefs, you can realize God within your own body."

Baba Sawan Singh made the teachings of Guru Nanak reach every home in India. Even though he did not go to the West in his physical form, in the form of Shabd that great Saint gave *darshan*[1] to many dear souls in the West. In the form of Shabd he pulled those souls and told them where he was residing. After coming into this world, the same great *Satguru*[2] made us understand how we have become lost and become separated from God, how we have to search for him, how we can meet God, and how to live our lives. He told us, "You people are looking for him outside, but you will not be able to find him because he is not anywhere outside."

Baba Sawan Singh Ji also gave the duty to Baba Somanath Ji to do that work in the southern part of India. Every Saint has his own way of doing things; only he knows whom he has to make work and in what way he has to make a certain being work. You all know the history of Baba Somanath Ji, how much sacrifice he made in his life. It is very easy to criticize any Mahatma, but to work as hard as he did and to live a life like that of a Mahatma is very difficult. If God could be realized without working hard, then what was the need for the Mahatmas to work hard?

You know that Baba Sawan Singh Ji would not come out from his meditation room for many days. He would sleep and eat very little. Once in the satsang Baba Sawan Singh Ji said, "I did not do anything. It is all the grace of Baba Jaimal Singh Ji." Banta Singh, who used to cook food for Baba Sawan Singh, was there and he said, "Master, then what were you doing bearing the hunger and thirst for so many days? When you would not come out from your room, when you would just stay there and meditate, what was that?" Sometimes the lovers of the Masters say such things. Guru Nanak had bedding which was made of stones and pebbles, and sitting on that he meditated for eleven years. Kabir Sahib also lived his life very simply. I have often said that before you take the refuge of any mahatma, you should first check to see whether he has done any hard work, any sacrifice, any meditation in his life or not.

Kabir Sahib says, "You should shave the head of the mother of such a guru who cannot remove your illusion." In the East there used to be a

---

[1] A gracious glance from a spiritual figure.

[2] Literally "True Guru"; a perfect Master, a fully realized soul who has been commissioned by God to teach the inner path to seekers after truth.

The Pain of Separation

general practice of shaving the head of a widow so that people would know that she could not bear any more children because her husband was dead. About such a guru's mother, Kabir says, "Why didn't she become a widow before giving birth to a person who became a false master? It would have been much better for her to remain infertile, because he would not have been born, and could not have deluded people by acting and posing." I often say that a prostitute is better than a hypocrite *sadhu* (renunciate) because she does not deceive anyone. She has a sign saying, "This is my reality; I do this work."

Kabir Sahib says that such a guru is involved in the Vedas himself and he allows his disciples to be swept away in the Vedas and Shastras. Such a master does not understand what the Vedas, Shastras and other religious scriptures say, and according to his limited understanding, he teaches his disciples about those religious scriptures. He does not have any right to go within, he does not have any power to go within, and he does not have any competence to take his disciples within.

So that great Almighty Satguru Sawan Singh told Baba Somanath Ji, "You should awaken the souls in South India; connect them with God Almighty and make them do the meditation of Naam." He gave the duty of going into the rest of the world to Master Kirpal Singh Ji. He told him, "You have to awaken the souls all over the world." Even though Master Sawan Singh had never been to the West in his physical form, still he had a vision in which he had seen Master Kirpal Singh Ji doing satsang for the Westerners. Sawan Singh Ji had said, "Yes, that is true, the time will come and that will happen." So, I mean to say that no curse affects the truth. That great Saint, Master Kirpal Singh Ji, went everywhere in the world; there is no peak of any mountain where he did not go and there is no depth of any water where he did not glorify the name of his Master Sawan Singh. He sang his praises all the time; whether he was sitting or standing, awake or asleep, he always sang the praises of his Master.

Kabir Sahib says that the sky is on fire, and fire is coming down from the sky. If there were no Saints in this world, this whole world would have burned down. God Almighty always comes into this world, and through the Saints and Mahatmas he protects his souls; he connects the fortunate with himself. Master Sawan Singh Ji used to say, "As are the parents, so are the children." Whatever the parents are like, the children also become like them. He used to give an example of a princess who fell in love with a prince, but their parents did not agree about their marriage. So, the princess said, "There is no need to hesitate in this matter, I will come tonight, and we will go to some other place. Then we will get married and live together." That night the princess brought a she-camel with her. Early in the morning they started their journey. On the way there was a small water course which they had to cross. When the she-camel came near that water course, the princess said, "Pull the rein, otherwise she will sit in the water." She added, "Her mother also had this same habit of sitting in the water."

There is always some time when such a thought comes into our mind which can change our thinking. When the prince heard that the she-camel and her mother both had the same habits, at once a thought came into his mind, "If the children of animals have the same habits as their parents, can that not be true also with human beings? In the future, when we have children, the girl who will be born of this woman may also run away with someone just as her mother is now doing with me. Then people would start saying my character also is not good." So, he thought of returning to his home. He told the princess, "There is something very important which I have forgotten in the palace; we should go back and get it." When they came back to the palace, he told the princess, "Look here, O Dear One, we were going to do a very bad karma[3] by running away without the permission of our parents. You would have been defamed; I would have been defamed also. There would not be any good for anyone and our children would have had habits like ours. Now you go to your palace and I will go to mine."

While here, I will be doing satsangs on the *banis* (verses) of Sufi Saint Sheikh Farid every day. All of you should listen carefully. You should pay

---

[3] The law of action and reaction which governs the fate of each person. Also used as a term for a given action which creates karma, or for fate, the result of previous actions. See also *Life and Death* by Kirpal Singh for an in-depth explanation.

The Pain of Separation

attention to it. Sheikh Farid got the inspiration to do the devotion of God from his mother. His mother was an initiate and when Sheikh Farid was a child playing, his mother would always tell him, "Dear son, you should do the devotion of the Lord; it is good to devote yourself to God." Sheikh Farid would ask her, "Mother, what is the use of doing the devotion of God? Will God give me sugar to do his devotion? Will he give me honey or jaggery to eat?" His mother said, "Yes, if we do the devotion of God, we do not need to beg for anything, because he gives us sweets, he gives us everything, because he does everybody's work." We know that in the beginning it is very difficult to taste the fruit of devotion. But later on, if we have devoted ourselves to the path, it becomes very difficult for us to go away from this path.

In their early days, the Mahatmas had to face many difficulties. But once they tasted the fruit of devotion, they could not disconnect themselves from this path. They faced all difficulties which came in their way happily. So, for the first few days Sheikh Farid's mother had to spread the prayer mat for him, make him sit for meditation and tell him that God has left some sugar for him. This went on for a few days, and she had to work hard. But afterwards, because she also gave him her attention, his soul started going within. So once Sheikh Farid's mother told him to get up from meditation, saying, "Get up dear son, God has left some sugar for you." When Sheikh Farid came out from that meditation, he said, "Mother, sugar, jaggery, honey, milk, these things are very sweet, but they do not reach anywhere near the sweetness of God. The taste which I had today from Naam is so sweet that that taste cannot be found in any of the other sweet things. That sweetness is forever." In his lifetime he became practically successful in the path and he gave the teachings of the path to many people. I will be giving satsangs on the bani of Sheikh Farid.

Once there was a woman who had five sons. She told her sons, "Dear children, it is difficult to make a living from those worldly businesses like farming or trading. Your father and I have been stealing and robbing because it is easy." So, she taught them the ways of stealing. She told them that people usually do not suspect women. Usually women have the habit of talking and showing off their valuable things like jewelry, etc. So, she would go to people's homes, talk to the women, and find out where they kept their jewelry or other valuables. Then she would leave a mark on that house, and also mark that particular place where the valuables were kept. She would also leave some asafetida[4] over there. Then she would come back and tell her children, "Dear sons, go into the house where you smell the asafetida, to the place I have marked, and get those valuables." Then the children would go and steal things from that house. So, you can see how the mother taught them to be thieves and robbers.

The meaning of this story is that when we give up the path of Shabd Naam, when we give up doing the meditation of Shabd Naam, then within us *hungatha* or egoism is created. (Hungatha comes from asafetida and denotes a bad smell but also egoism.) From that hungatha or egoism comes a bad smell.

Who are the thieves? These five passions: lust, anger, greed, attachment and egoism are the five thieves. They come and plunder us. That is why Kabir said, "O Travelers, remain awake because thieves come into the town. When they see anyone being careless, they at once take away their bags." That is why he said to remain awake, alert. Guru Nanak Sahib also said, "Awake, O People, awake; this traveler has left." He said, "O Dear Ones, you should become awake in this world, because your friends, your fellow travelers, have left this world. Finish your work before you also have to leave." That is why Sheikh Farid says that when egoism comes, the five thieves also come in and plunder us.

In this bani Sheikh Farid will explain to us many different things, giving us many beautiful examples. We should listen to it carefully and pay attention to it.

The day the bride is to be wedded is predetermined.
And on that day, the Angel of Death, of whom you have heard, comes and shows his face to you.

---

[4] A resinous gum with a very pungent odor, used as a spice in Indian cooking or as a digestive aid

The Pain of Separation

Sheikh Farid says when our soul enters this body, God Almighty fixes the time of her departure. At that fixed time the Angel of Death comes and shows us his face, saying, "Now I have come to take you." Mahatmas have called that being, who comes to take our soul at the time of its departure from the body, by many different names. At some places he is called the Lord of Judgment, at some places he is called the Angel of Death, and at other places he is called the God of Death.

In India it is a general practice that when one wants to get one's daughter married, one fixes the date of the wedding and on that day the man comes to marry her. The groom takes the bride away even if she is not ready, even if she cries a lot. No matter what she says or does, he does not have any pity on her; he will take her away at the fixed time.

Hazrat Waris Shah wrote the story of the great lovers Hir and Ranjha. Hir was married to Kayra, even though she did not want it, because her parents wanted her to marry him. Hazrat Waris Shah said that our soul is like Hir and the Angel of Death is like Kayra. As soon as the Angel of Death gets his hands on the soul, he runs away with her, just as Kayra took Hir away even though she didn't want to go with him. When the Angel of Death comes, he does not wait. He does not care whether the bride is ready or not, because the day was fixed ahead of time. Farid Sahib says, "On that day when your soul entered the body, that particular day and place when the Angel of Death will come for her was arranged."

There are only two powers which come to take the soul. The Shabd Guru will come, if we have received Naam initiation, because he has to protect our soul. But if we do not have the Master and Naam, then the Angel of Death will come to take us away.

In our lives we see many incidents when dear souls who do the meditation are about to leave the body. Many days before their departure from this world they tell us what date they are going to leave the body. *Satsangis*[5]

---

[5] A term used to refer to a disciple of a true Master, or any seeker after truth. Literally "one who attends satsang."

who go very high in meditation will tell us many months in advance when they have to go.

There was an initiate of Baba Sawan Singh whose name was Sunder Das who lived with me for twenty years. He was a very good meditator. We would sit at our farm, after lighting a fire to keep us warm, and we would meditate for eight hours at a stretch. One day while meditating, a piece of burning wood fell out from the fire and burned his leg, but he did not realize that it had happened. When he got up from meditation, he told me, "The intoxication which I have received today will never come again."

A couple of months before he left the body, he told us, "Baba Sawan Singh and Master Kirpal Singh will come to take me on a certain day." He prepared his coffin himself, ahead of time. He left the body in the presence of many satsangis. A few hours before he left the body, he said, "Now the court of the Lord is open, and I want to take my sister along with me also." But when his sister heard this, since she was not an initiate, she was afraid of death.

Now you see that with satsangis there is so much happiness at the time of departure from this world. Not even on the day of his wedding does he have that much happiness. Because when a person is going to get married, somewhere in his mind, he thinks that he is going to fall into a trap. He thinks he will be more attached to this world after the wedding.

Mahatmas do not tell us anything from hearsay. We come across so many incidents in our lifetime of how disciples initiated by the perfect Masters are protected by the Master at the time of death. The Negative Power cannot come to bother souls initiated by perfect Masters. This is the truth of the perfect Masters. That is how they protect disciples within and without.

It has been quite a long time since Master Sawan Singh Ji left his physical body, but even now he is protecting and taking care of his souls. In the same way, many years have passed since our beloved Master Kirpal finished his earthly sojourn and went back to his real home, but still there are so many examples of how he is protecting and taking care of his souls. The truth does not need any evidence. I receive so many telegrams,

The Pain of Separation

so many cables, so many letters from dear ones, in which people write how they felt the presence of the Master and his protection when their near and dear one was leaving the body. What to speak of human souls, Masters even shower grace on the animals of satsangis when they leave the body.

The Angel of Death forces the poor soul out, breaking the bones.
Make the soul understand, no one can challenge the writ of God.

Now he says that the Angel of Death will not have any enmity towards anyone, but he just comes at the fixed time for everyone. If someone has prepared for his departure ahead of time, he does not feel any pain, he does not have any difficulty in leaving the body. If the Master has come, such a soul goes with the Master happily. If someone has not prepared himself for the time of departure, then it is very painful and difficult for him.

Guru Arjan Dev Ji Maharaj says that the dying one twists his hands, moves his body, and changes color. If the person has not prepared himself for the time of death, in the pain of that difficult time, he moves his body here and there; he suffers a great deal of pain. Sometimes he calls for a good doctor, sometimes he calls his sons and family. In that moment of pain, he changes his mind so many, times but no one comes to his rescue.

Usually the family members of Saints and Mahatmas do not believe in them. They do not take any advantage of their coming into this world. My family always said that Kirpal had done some magic on my head because I had left a lot of worldly property when Master instructed me to do so. I would laugh and tell them, "Kirpal did not take any property with him; it is still there," and, "Maybe you are right; he has done some magic on my head." They opposed me so much that I had to finish all my worldly relations with them. But I did tell them that my beloved Master used to say that Master protects even the souls of the animals of satsangis. I told them, "That great Power will definitely protect your souls and he will come to your rescue when you leave your bodies."

On the Soul's Wedding Day

In July my elder brother was about to leave the body. He had not been sick at all; he left the body without any sickness. But before leaving the body he said, "There are four butchers who are holding me from all four sides, and they are giving me pain." You can imagine who those butchers were and why they came. He called out, "The butchers have caught me." But soon after, he uttered the name of my beloved Master and said, "Now he has come, and he is protecting me." Before leaving the body, he told the rest of the family members that they should get initiation. You can see how that great power came and rescued him.

Similarly, there is one dear one who does *sevā*[6] at our ashram, Sardar Verik. He used to confuse other people and make them fight with each other. His father had the same habit. When his father's end time came, he said, "They are beating me on my back with heated iron bars." Verik had told us that he and his brother were standing near him and they both saw the signs of the heated iron bars on his back. But a few days later when their mother, who was an initiate, left the body, she said, "Sprinkle water and make way for the Master. He is coming to take me." They said, "But we cannot see the Master." She replied, "You do not have the eyes to see him."

You see, although they were married, the husband and wife did not have the same kind of karma; they left the body under different circumstances and in different ways. Master Sawan Singh Ji also used to say that not even the karmas of the husband and wife are equal. Everyone has his own karmas to suffer. That is why Farid Sahib lovingly tells us that if someone has not prepared himself for that time when death is going to come, then he will suffer a lot of pain and difficulties. It is one thing, when we are living, to say, "What is the need of the Master; what is the need of receiving Naam initiation?" But when the fixed time comes, the Angel of Death does not spare anyone. When the person is leaving the body, he lies there while the mother, father, sisters and brothers stand next to him crying, but no one can help.

---

[6] Selfless service in a spiritual cause.

The Pain of Separation

Kabir Sahib says, "O Man, you came into this world crying, because you were disconnected from Almighty Lord, but everyone else was happy and laughing. You should achieve such a thing that you may leave this world laughing." If we could achieve such a thing in our lifetime which would give us everlasting happiness, then at the time of our leaving this world, we would go happily and laughing. Our parents and relatives would cry when we leave, but we would not be affected by those weeping.

The soul is the bride, Death is the groom who takes her away after marrying her.

After the wedding, the groom takes the bride away, even though she cries a lot; she complains and refuses, but still she has to go. She cannot find anyone's support. In the same way, when our soul leaves the body she cries and suffers pain. If she has not prepared herself for that fixed time, she finds it very difficult, but there is no one there who can help her. Tulsi Sahib says, "At the time of death the person keeps on looking at his past and his eyes shed tears. O Brothers, who can help him then?"

He has the pain of separation from his relatives and he cannot tell them what he is going through within. He stares at one place and the family becomes worried. Even the doctors say, "There is not much hope left, now you can take him home." By giving the example of the bride who is taken away by the groom, Farid Sahib has lovingly explained to us what happens to our soul at the fixed time of her departure from this body, if she has not prepared herself for that time.

The body, after bidding farewell to the soul, whom will she now embrace?

He says that only they are wise who appreciate the time and prepare in time to spare themselves from death. How can we spare ourselves from death? When death happens, at that time, first our feet become numb, and

On the Soul's Wedding Day

we feel that no life is left in our feet. That feeling of not having life goes on moving upwards in our body. It starts from our feet, and soon we say that we do not have any life in our waist. As it progresses upwards, we say that there is no circulation of blood in our arms. After it leaves all the lower parts of the body, and comes to our throat center, we say now we hear only our cough. Guru Nanak Sahib says, "When our soul comes to the throat center, after withdrawing herself from all lower parts of the body, if we remember some perfect Master and our attention goes to the Naam, even at that time our soul can still be protected from the Angel of Death." So, if we had prepared ourselves before the time of death, if we had learned how to withdraw our soul from all the parts of the body and come to the eye center, we would not feel any difficulty and pain when our death happens. Guru Nanak says, "You should go to that house, while living, where you have to go after death."

The Path is finer than a hair; have you not heard of it?
O Farid, not even an ant can walk it; do not stand unaware.

He says, "Look here, O Dear One, the path on which you have to travel is very thin, thinner than a hair, and sharper than a razor. It is full of difficulties and pains." He says, "I am sorry that even though many Mahatmas came and asked us why we were asleep in the worldly pleasures, why we were not listening to the voice of God, still we have not taken their advice." Farid Sahib very lovingly says that the path is sharper than the edge of a sword, much thinner than a hair. This is the path on which you will travel on your way back, and on that journey, you will not have any companion. You will have to go there by yourself.

O Farid, it is hard to become a God's man, as my ways are worldly.
On my head I am carrying a load of sins. Where can I take it?

Now very lovingly he says that we all receive Naam initiation and become satsangis. In the name of Almighty Lord, we accept *fakiri,* the ways

The Pain of Separation

of the *fakirs*.[7] We act like fakirs. "But," he asks, "who is the real fakir? Only he who does the meditation of Naam and reaches the home of the Lord is the real fakir."

He who connects himself with God Almighty is the fakir. Swami Ji Maharaj says, "I call him a Saint who makes his soul reach Sat Lok. He who has made his soul reach Sach Khand is the Saint." Kabir Sahib says, "There is no difference between the Lord and the Saint, because the Saint has finished his search and has realized the Oversoul. After meeting God Almighty, he also becomes the form of God."

When we come to the path and accept its teachings, we say that we will become fakirs, great meditators; we will not get involved in worldly pursuits and pleasures. But if we give up the path of Naam and do the worldly things which we were doing before, it becomes very embarrassing for us. Then we become even worse than the worldly people. We come back into the world carrying a heavier burden of karmas on our head. Our friends in the community even taunt us saying, "Until yesterday, he had become a sadhu, now he has come back like one of us."

To accept the Saints' teachings and become like the Saints is not an easy thing. It is very difficult to do, and before one tries to do this, he needs to think about it a lot. One needs to think about its consequences for many days, for many months; I would even say that one needs to think about it for many years before he steps into this. Guru Nanak says that the heart of a Saint or a Fakir is like the heart of a tree. No matter whether one gives water to the tree or cuts its roots, it does not take away its shade from anyone.

Hazrat Bahu says, "When a person is throwing things at you, it is up to him whether he throws a mango, an orange, or just the skins of fruits at you. He could even throw dirty things upon you." Kabir Sahib says, "Some people come to the Master with devotion. Some people come with ill feelings. But Saints welcome both of them alike." They do not pay any attention to the ill feelings of anyone.

---

[7] A Muslim term for a renunciate or Saint.

On the Soul's Wedding Day

Baba Sawan Singh Ji used to say that some people come to satsang out of habit, some people come for Naam initiation, and others to give food to their soul; but some people only come to satsang to steal people's shoes. However, Saints and Mahatmas welcome everyone alike. They look at everyone with the same eyes and they love all. They do not care about the intentions of the person who comes. Farid Sahib lovingly says that when we carry the burden of our sins on our head, we become exactly the same as we were before.

For a few days, when we have yearning, we get up in the night, sit for meditation and do all the good things. However, later on when the mind attacks and we let him defeat us, then we become lazy and we do not meditate. Swami Ji Maharaj says, "Those who are thieves of meditation suffer so many difficulties and pain. Laziness and sleep bother them and every day they live in illusion." They get kicked and knocked by lust and anger, and they are drowned in the river of delusion. Their mind becomes the slave of one thing or another. So lovingly Farid Sahib says, "It is very difficult to become a Saint; it is very difficult to accept the fakir. One needs to think about it a lot."

Farid Sahib had done a lot of sacrifice in his life; he had performed many austerities. For twelve years of his life he had wandered here and there in the forest; he had borne a lot of hunger and thirst in his life. When someone becomes a sadhu and is searching for God, at that time he gives up all worldly pleasures and comforts. But in this age, life is in the food, so it is very difficult to give up food.

At one place Farid Sahib has written, "O Farid, hunger is worse than death. Even if you have eaten the night before, next morning when you awake hunger is still there, and you have to eat again." Once when he was going somewhere, he felt hungry and he saw some melons growing in a garden. He asked the gardener to give him some melons, but that man said, "Why should I give you melons? What kind of fakir are you? You have become a fakir and still you are desiring melons!"

Farid did not reply to that gardener. Instead he cursed his own self, because his mind had desired melons. He felt very sorry for himself and he thought, "It is a pity that I could not even fulfill my own desires. If I

The Pain of Separation

had worked hard at some job, I would have easily fulfilled all the desires of my body. If I had worked hard, I could have even fulfilled the desires of others. But since I have lived in the forest, this is my condition that I have to bear the taunts and criticisms of others." With these kind of thoughts Farid Sahib went away.

After he left that garden, in God's will a change happened; all the melons which were growing in that garden became people's heads. When the caretaker saw that the melons had become heads, he was afraid the owner of the garden would be upset with him. After some time, the owner came and asked the gardener how the melons had turned into people's heads. The gardener said, "Sir, I don't know why this happened, but one fakir came and asked me to give him some melons. I did not give him any melons, and he went away cursing himself." So that farmer went to Sheikh Farid and requested, "My Lord, all the melons have turned into human heads. I don't know how I will bear this loss. I don't even own the land where the melons were growing; I rented that from somebody else. I have to pay rent and pay workers who look after the garden. Now how will I make the payments? I am a poor person and my children will starve if I do not make money from this garden. Kindly shower grace on me."

Farid Sahib then smiled and said, "Dear one, you may have been mistaken. You should go back and see. All the melons are there." Farid Sahib also told him that one melon would remain as a head. Then that farmer asked Sheikh Farid to tell him the reason why all the melons became people's heads. Farid Sahib told him, "Go back to your garden and ask that melon which is in the form of a head. Ask him why all this happened. He will answer your question."

When the farmer went back to his garden, he saw that all the melons were there except for one which had remained a head. He went to that head and asked, "Tell me why all these melons were turned into heads." The head replied, "God was going to shower a lot of grace on us; that is why that fakir was going to eat us. With our very good fate, we melons were going to go into the body of that Saint. Then God Almighty was going to reward us; he was going to give us liberation from this type of body. That is why we had become heads. Only because of the grace of God Almighty were we going to be released from the bodies of melons."

Master Sawan Singh Ji used to say that this is a concession which Saints and Mahatmas get from God Almighty: whatever animal they ride is released from the cycle of eighty-four *lakhs*[8] births and deaths. It definitely gets liberated and gets a human birth in which to do devotion. In the same way, if they eat the fruit of any tree, the tree also gets a concession; that tree also gets an opportunity to go into a human body. The soul in that tree escapes from the cycle of eighty-four lakhs births and deaths. Further, anything which comes in contact with a Saint gets such a concession.

The melon said, "God Almighty showered grace on us and all this happened." He said, "Many times we came in the bodies of melons. Many times you people ate us and we went into your stomachs; many times you became the melons and we sold you in the market. This was a very good opportunity for all of us to get liberation from this coming and going." After the farmer heard that he repented a lot. He wished that Farid Sahib had eaten those melons and he would also have gotten liberation from the cycle of coming and going in this world.

This is why Saints and Mahatmas, the Beloveds of God, say that fakiri, the Way of the Saints, is not a very little thing; it is not an easy thing to adopt. It is a very difficult thing; it is a very high thing. Only he is a fakir who, in spite of getting all things from God Almighty, still remains patient and uses things within limits. The Mahatmas of very high order came into this world. Many people opposed and criticized them and tortured them, but still they did not curse anyone. They did not think ill of others. They always gave them love. Kabir Sahib says that it is better to fight with the Sadhu than to be in love with the *manmukh*.[9] Because our fighting with the Sadhu will liberate us, whereas our love for the manmukh will only take us

---

[8] A term meaning one hundred thousand. The "eight-four lakhs" refers to the cycle of incarnations through the eighty-four hundred thousand species.

[9] Literally, "mouthpiece of the mind", one who is under the control of the mind and is worldly minded.

The Pain of Separation

in the cycle of eighty-four lakhs births and deaths. It is said that the anger of a Sadhu is just like boiling milk. The anger of the world is destructive, but even from the anger of a Sadhu we can get a lot of grace. That is why here he lovingly says that fakiri is not a very small thing.

I don't know what to do. The world is a hidden fire.

Now Farid Sahib says that the whole world is burning in a hidden, subtle fire. What is that hidden fire? The desires and pleasures of the sense organs make the soul dance like a monkey. But from outside no smoke can be seen coming from this hidden, subtle fire. So here Farid Sahib lovingly says, "God Almighty has showered a lot of grace on me, he has saved me from this hidden fire. I was very fortunate that God Almighty brought me in contact with my Master and he has saved me from this fire."

My Lord did good, otherwise I too would have burned.

O Farid, had I known the days were few, I would have used them carefully. Had I known my Lord was innocent of nature, I would have had less pride.

In fact, Farid Sahib became practically successful and he achieved liberation while living. But in order to make us understand, he says, "If I had known that breaths are limited, and we do not have much time here, I would have appreciated this life more. I would have used these breaths only for appropriate things; I would have done the devotion of the Lord." He says, "If I had known that God belongs to the poor ones, the humble ones, the meek ones, then after coming into this body, I would not have had pride of anything. I would have remained humble." Farid Sahib has told us in this bani that our life is very precious; we cannot get this human birth at any cost. This body is very precious; we cannot get any part of this body at any cost. So why not utilize the body which we have been given? Do the devotion of the Lord. Why not devote all available time to the devotion of the Lord, and use all our breaths for his remembrance? We should spend all our time in *simran*,[10] whether we are sitting or standing, walking, talking or doing anything. All the breaths which we breathe out should be accompanied by simran so that every single breath is devoted to the Lord because we do not know whether we will get such an opportunity again or not.

---

[10] Literally, remembrance. Used for remembrance of the Lord. Also repetition of a mantra, such as that given by a true Master at the time of initiation.

Chapter 2

The Disease of Yearning

Last night in satsang I said that all this blooming garden, all this grace, is from that great Emperor of Emperors, Almighty Baba Sawan Singh. I tried to tell you how lovingly Baba Sawan Singh Ji used to explain things to us, giving us those examples which are of practical use in our day-to-day life. Whenever Saints and Mahatmas come into this world, they have used examples of those things to which we are attached. They explain to us the reality of our life, using those various examples.

Baba Sawan Singh Ji used to give the example of a prince who did not have any interest in studying. The king and queen were very worried about him because that prince fell into bad company and lost his interest in gaining an education. His parents were worried how he would be able to rule over the kingdom. They hired many good teachers to teach him, but no one was successful in giving him any education. Finally, when they were tired of trying so many different teachers, someone suggested, "Why don't you go to a Mahatma, because the suggestions of Mahatmas are unique, and they have their own ways of making a person understand things." Mahatmas can easily solve those puzzles which we worldly people cannot solve. Because they are experienced beings, with their experience and love they solve all the problems which we cannot solve ourselves.

So, the king went to a Mahatma and told him, "Master, my son doesn't study. How will he be able to be a ruler? It is a big responsibility being

The Pain of Separation

a king. I do not know how he will be able to enjoy his power and rule over the kingdom without an education." The Mahatma told him, "Don't worry. Leave him with me and I will make him study."

After the Mahatma accepted the prince, first he thought, "I should try to find out his habits and the things which interest him." He called the prince and asked him, "Dear son, tell me what you like most." The boy replied, "I like to feed pigeons and make them fly." The Mahatma said, "Okay, we will go and buy some pigeons and we will take care of them." He also added, "In my childhood, I used to do the same thing."

When they bought some pigeons, the Mahatma said, "This is not enough, we should buy some more." So, they bought a lot of pigeons. After they had bought all those pigeons the Mahatma said, "Dear son, now we have so many pigeons to look after and if we do not give them any names to identify them, then it will be difficult for us to enjoy them. If one is sick, how will we know which one, unless we name them? How will we know who is flying unless they have names by which we can call them?"

The prince agreed to that, because this was a hobby he was interested in, so he agreed to the suggestion of the Mahatma that the pigeons should be named. The Mahatma named those pigeons with letters of the alphabet. He called one A, he called one B, and some other he called C. He went on naming the pigeons A, B, C, D, E, and all the other letters of the alphabet. But there were too many pigeons, so after all the letters were used up, the Mahatma said, "We still have some pigeons left." Then he started forming words using different letters and, in that way, he started to make the prince remember the alphabet.

In this way he gradually taught the alphabet to the prince and he also taught him how to join letters to form a word. He taught him how to read the words formed by the letters. When he started learning to read, the Mahatma gave him a small book containing some good stories for children which he read and enjoyed. This went on for some time and as the prince grew up, he started understanding the importance of studying and he gained an interest in education. In this way he gave up his habit of playing with pigeons, and he started having interest in gaining worldly knowledge.

The Disease of Yearning

So Master Sawan Singh Ji used to say that Saints and Mahatmas have so many different suggestions and so many ways of making the soul understand. When a *jiva* (soul) comes to a Master Saint, the Master can easily see what interests that person has and what thing he likes the most. Master can easily see what sickness that person has and what kind of medicine he needs.

Last night in satsang I told how Sufi Saint Sheikh Farid connected us with spirituality by giving us various worldly examples. Once a person who had a jewel in his pocket went into the market to sell it. But as he was carrying that jewel, maybe he did not keep it in a good way and he lost it somewhere. When he got to the marketplace, he could not find the jewel in his pocket. He became very afraid and worried. Sometimes such incidents happen to us also when we lose something valuable, some money, gold or some very precious jewel, because of our carelessness. When we realize that it is not there then we are afraid and we worry about it. We are sad but we do not ask ourselves why we lost that valuable thing.

That person who had lost his jewel came upon Sheikh Farid not far from where he had lost his jewel. He told Sheikh Farid, "Master, you should tell me where I have lost my jewel. Because Mahatmas have the quality of all-consciousness, and you must know where I have lost it, so please tell me where it is."

Sheikh Farid replied, "Dear one, you lost that jewel because of your carelessness. Because you did not appreciate its value, you did not protect it well. If you had understood its value, if you had taken care of it, you would have never lost it." This is a worldly example that he gave; he lovingly told that dear one who had lost his jewel, "Dear one, the human birth which you have been given is also very precious. It is more precious than that jewel. It is priceless. If you had realized that it is priceless and that you will not get this again at any cost, then you would have protected it. When you see that your human birth is passing without being used for the purpose for which it was given, when you see that it is being wasted, and if you had realized that, then you would have fallen in love with the Master very strongly. You would have loved him very much, so that this birth might become successful and you would have taken advantage of this precious jewel."

The Pain of Separation

Had I known my ties with you would break, I would have tightened the knots.
I have searched the whole world, but no one is like you.

He says that if we had realized the value of this human birth, we would have fastened the knot of our love with the Master very tightly. Just as we chain things so that we may be sure that we will not lose them, we would have fastened this knot of the love of the Master very strongly. He says, "I have wandered everywhere in this world but I have not found even one person like you, O My Satguru."

O Farid, if you are of good intellect, do not write the black deeds,
Bowing your head, look under your collar, (within).

We know that in our day-to-day life we sometimes have to deal with the government administration. Once Sheikh Farid had to go to court. There he saw that a clerk who was making judgments was taking bribes from people, and then he would decide cases in their favor. This was the first time Sheikh Farid had visited a place where somebody accepted bribes to do something illegal. Sheikh Farid wrote this couplet to that person who accepted the bribes. He says, "O Dear One, if you are so wise and clever, why pollute your soul by accepting bribes from people? Why blacken your own record sheet when you know that you will have to pay the consequences of your karmas? O Dear One, look within and see who will pay off these karmas you have created; who will settle your accounts?"

O Farid, do not hit them back who give you blows.
Kiss the feet of those who come to your door.

Farid Sahib spent a major part of his life in the forest doing his meditation and performing austerities. Once when he was meditating in the forest, an egotistic person came there; since Farid Sahib was meditating, he did not see him coming. You know that the meditators always keep death in front of their eyes. They always remember death. So, when that person asked Farid Sahib, "Which road goes to the town?" Farid Sahib pointed to a graveyard and told him, "This is the road which goes to town." When that

The Disease of Yearning

person went on that road, he found only the graveyard and he saw only graves. Then he thought that maybe that Mahatma had played a joke on him and he thought of giving him a beating and teaching him a lesson. He came back and slapped Farid Sahib. Farid Sahib did not complain; he did not react violently. He just said, "In the love of God," and kept smiling.

That person who had slapped Farid Sahib said, "Mahatma Ji, I gave you such a beating but still you did not stop me, you did not complain." Farid Sahib replied, "Dear one, what I told you is true, 'The grave is the real city.' The grave is the only place where we all must reside; that is our permanent abode. That is the real city. The reason I did not react violently was that the Beloveds of God have a unique kind of humility within them. They do not beat the person who slaps them. They do not respond to the throwing of a stone with a brick. Instead of cursing those who have beaten them, the Mahatmas wish them well."

Master Sawan Singh Ji used to say that such a kind of humility can also be a deceptive thing. Because if we are keeping quiet and suffering such kinds of tortures for our own self-interest, then it is like deceiving ourselves as well as others. Mahatmas lovingly tell us that if we have humility it should be true humility, it should be pure humility, it should be the highest humility. They say that God accepts only that kind of humility. That is why Mahatmas lovingly say that you should never think ill of the Masters.

We know that only one who is greedy thinks ill of others; only he goes to beat up or to harm someone. And only one who is greedy or who has some selfish motive is afraid of other people. Guru Nanak Dev Ji Maharaj says that Master souls never intimidate anyone and they are not intimidated by anyone. They are afraid of only one power, their Master. They are always afraid lest they should do anything that would displease the Master, or which might become the cause of insults to their Master, because there is a saying that if the dog is bad its owner is blamed.

O Farid, when it was your time to earn God, you were involved in the world. Now when your death has overpowered you, your carriage must go along, with whatever is loaded on it.

The Pain of Separation

Farid Sahib makes us understand, saying, "O Dear One, when you had an opportunity to do the devotion of the Lord, when you had your youth and you were capable of doing the devotion of the Lord and realizing him, at that time you remained involved in worldly pleasures, and in gaining name and fame and the praises of the world. Now, when old age has come and death stands in front of you, then you think, 'Now I should somehow do something to please God Almighty; now I should do the devotion of the Lord.'" Baba Jalan Jat, a great meditator in the town called Nowshera, used to say, "When we were young, we took care of the cows. When we grew up, we plowed the fields. Now in our old age we are moving the rosary and, in that way, we say we are doing a favor to God." If we start doing the devotion of the Lord in our old age it is only to tell God, "Now we are doing your devotion; you should not say that we did not devote ourselves to you, that we did not remember you." So just to be good in front of God and just to make ourselves look good we do the devotion, but that is in name only.

Old people have so many burdens on their heads. When they sit for meditation, they have many worries, many things to think about. Sometimes their attention goes to their family or their children. It is very difficult for an old person to do meditation. When one sits in meditation in old age, he feels that he is caught somewhere between the world and God.

Swami Ji Maharaj says that the foolish one is carrying the burden and now he has become afraid of the pains. No one told him to carry the burden; he himself chose to carry it. Now he has become nervous because it is very painful and difficult to continue carrying that burden. Someone says, "My son does not obey me," or "My daughter is not serving me." Someone else fights with his wife and if someone loses his son, then he becomes like a mad person.

Swami Ji Maharaj says that when old age comes, a person has so many worries, attachments and entanglements in this world that he cannot do the devotion of God. When his end time comes, even his family members say, "Now we should make you hear the Gita," or, "We should make you hear a recitation of the Sukhmani Sahib." At that time, they try to take his attention towards the devotion of God. But what can a person do at that

The Disease of Yearning

time when he has so many other worries and burdens in his mind? He was supposed to do all those things when he was in his youth. When a person is young and able, he should do the meditation then.

> *Look, Farid, what has happened: your beard has turned gray.*
> *The end has come nearer, the past is left behind far away.*

Farid Sahib lovingly says, "Look here, O Dear One, the hair on your head and your face has turned white. It has become very white. This is a sign that the early stages of life have passed; now you are in the last stage of your life. Your childhood has gone, your youth has gone, and now old age is standing in front of you." Guru Nanak says, "The warning from the Angels of Death comes in the form of white hair which grows near our ears; now a person is imprisoned in the chains of *maya*.[1]" Whether one is a man or a woman, first of all the hair near the ears starts becoming gray, then white, and that is a sign that old age has come.

When the hair near the ears becomes white it is like someone is whispering in our ear, "O man, you have spoiled your youth; now at least in your old age, do the meditation." But at that time, instead of learning a lesson from that warning, we dye our white hairs and make them black again. But the Angel of Death will not be deceived; he will definitely come at the appropriate time. Here Farid says that your breaths are limited, you are losing your breaths, yet your desires are increasing.

If one has Master and Naam initiation, even in meditation he will ask his Master to give him this thing and that thing. He goes on asking for worldly things from the Master. If Master would fulfill all our worldly desires, he could never liberate us even if he tried for millions of births, because we create and get attached to so many desires that it is too much even for the Master. It is too much for us to come out from that trap of desires.

Our relationship with the Masters is that of spirituality; they do not interfere with our worldly life. Of course, they tell us that we should work

---

[1] Illusion, the feminine aspect of Kal, separates the soul from God. Also used as a term for the material things of this world.

The Pain of Separation

hard, because one who works hard becomes successful, even in worldly work. Such a one becomes successful in the path of spirituality as well. So here Farid Sahib says, "The days which you have remaining to live have now come nearer to you, and the days which you have already lived have gone very far from you. Death is approaching and your youth has gone far away."

> *Look, Farid, what has happened: the sugar has become poison.*
> *To whom can we tell our pains except our Lord.*

Without meeting the Master and receiving Naam initiation, no matter how sweetly a person speaks, still he cannot become successful. It is all as useless as a parrot that has learned something and repeats it again and again. Farid Sahib says, "Now the pleasures which seemed as sweet as honey have no taste in them." When you indulge in pleasures again and again you lose interest; you lose the taste of them. At the time of death those pleasures bite you when the soul is about to leave the body. At that time a man cries, he suffers pain, he calls people for help, but no one can help him because he has not received initiation. If he does not have a Master, who can help him there? So now he says that the worldly pleasures which seemed very sweet when the person was indulging in them are like poison: they are very bitter and they give so much pain. Now where can he go, and who is the Master he can tell about his pain? He does not have any Lord or Master who would release him from the pains of the worldly pleasures which once gave happiness.

> *O Farid, after seeing, the eyes have dimmed; after hearing, the ears have become deaf.*
> *The branch has ripened and the leaves have withered.*

Now lovingly Farid Sahib says that, after seeing the colors of the world, his eyes have become weak. But they are not content and they still want to look at the plays of the world. The ears also, after hearing the sweet melodious sounds of the world, have become old. When a person

The Disease of Yearning

cannot hear, family members bring a hearing aid so that somehow, they can communicate with the old man. We still have the same ears through which we have heard the different melodies of the world. Our ears have enjoyed so many worldly sounds that they are content now; they are tired of listening to worldly things. But when the old man gets a hearing aid, he again wants to listen to worldly music. He wants to go to the cinema and listen to those sounds. He wants to go in bad company and listen to bad talk.

This is why Farid Sahib says that even though we know that when the crop is ready the farmer will harvest it, in the same way, when our eyes and ears refuse to work anymore for us, then we know that we have lost them all. But still we think that there is hope for our survival, still we think that we have a long life to live.

Regarding meditation he still has the same complaints: "My legs ache; my knees give me pain. I cannot concentrate at the eye center; my mind does not stay at one place." The meaning of Farid Sahib's verse is that even though our eyes, ears, and our bodies refuse to work, even though we have lost the ability to function normally, still as far as meditation is concerned, we are not ready to go in that direction. We are not ready to devote ourselves to God. Why do we not go towards the path of devotion? Because the forces of the Negative Power are always keeping us extroverted and they are deluding us. Our greatest enemy, our mind, never allows us to go within; he always keeps us outside.

Those who have not meditated in black, they hardly meditate in white.[2]
Love the Lord so that you may get the new color.

Farid Sahib says that even if we have lost our youth, as time slipped from our hands, and now we have come to old age, still wholeheartedly we should do the meditation of Naam. Even meditating in old age, you will be dyed in the color of Naam. Master Sawan Singh Ji always used to say,

---

[2] "In black" indicates when the hair is black, in youth, and "in white" indicates when the hair is white, in old age.

The Pain of Separation

"If God graciously gives us Naam initiation in our youth, we should take advantage of it. We should grab the sweet rice." This expression means that we should take advantage of the opportunity. It means that we should do the meditation; we should rise above the level of the mind and senses.

Farid Sahib says you should let the color of Naam fill you. If you have lost your youth, at least don't lose your old age. Even if you meditate in old age, your devotion will be accepted. That is why he says that no matter when one does the devotion and remembrance of Almighty Lord, God accepts that person's devotion.

You know that Dhru and Prahlad were devotees of God when they were very young and God Almighty gave them a place at his feet. Guru Amar Das Ji Maharaj was very old. He was almost seventy-two years old when he came to the feet of his Master, but wholeheartedly he did the seva of his Master. Whatever his Master ordered, he carried out wholeheartedly. He brought water for the *langar* (free community kitchen) of the Master. Being pleased with his seva and devotion his Master gave him the *gaddi* (throne) and the responsibility to become his successor. That is why Farid Sahib says that in whatever age of your life you remember him and do his devotion, he accepts it.

Shloka of Guru Amar Das:

O Farid, if one wants, he can remember the Lord in black as well as white.
But the Lord's love comes not to any who crave it.
Because this cup of love is of the Lord, he gives it to whomsoever he wishes.

Now this is the writing of Guru Amar Das Ji Maharaj, the third Guru in the Sikh line. The couplets of Guru Amar Das are also included with the bani of Sheikh Farid. Here Guru Amar Das says, "If one gets Naam initiation in his youth, it is very easy for him to do the devotion of God; it is easier for him to realize God in his youth than in his old age." The work which an old man takes a long time to do, a young man can do quickly. If an old man can sit straight without moving his body for two hours in meditation, a young man can keep his back straight for eight or ten hours.

The Disease of Yearning

He can meditate more. That is why he says that in youth it is not as difficult to do the devotion of God as it is in old age.

Guru Amar Das only got the opportunity to come to the Master in his old age, so he says we cannot control when we will get the love of the Master and Naam initiation. It is just a misunderstanding to think that we are capable of going to the Master anytime we want. In fact, it is the grace of the Master himself that brings us to his feet; God Almighty has kept this in his hand. Only he knows and only he decides to whom he will give this cup of love and when he will fill that cup of love for him. Only he knows whose time has come.

Often, I have said that God Almighty himself decides what soul is going to wander in this world more and what soul is going to get liberation. He alone makes the decision about which souls he has to connect with himself. Those souls who are going to get connected with God Almighty and those souls who are supposed to get liberation, only they come to the feet of the Master and get Naam initiation from him.

Often, I have said that for the Master it makes no difference whether he is far from the disciple or near. Either he will cross oceans and climb mountains to reach the disciple, or he will bring the disciple to his feet. This is something which he decides because he knows best who deserves initiation and who does not. Our Master Kirpal Singh Ji used to say that a person who is sitting on top of a mountain knows at what place fire is burning and what is happening down below. In the same way, the Mahatma who is sitting in Sach Khand knows in whose heart there is yearning for God and who wants to do his devotion. Only he who is sitting on top knows whose time has come and who is supposed to get the color of Naam. Our Supreme Father Kirpal used to say that it is difficult for a man to become a man; it is not difficult to realize God. He also used to say that God Almighty himself is searching for a true human being, for a sincere man.

Often, I have told you about my own life story that I had not heard anything about my Supreme Father Kirpal. I had neither heard any criticism of him nor any praise of him. I had never even come across any of his disciples, even though I had had the yearning to meet such a Mahatma

The Pain of Separation

ever since my childhood. In this search I came across Baba Bishan Das, who gave me initiation into the first Two Words.[3] In fact, he laid the foundation stone of my life.

For many years, sitting underground, I meditated on those Two Words, but the fact is that I was not content, I was still searching. There was a time when Baba Sawan Singh said, "The Mahatma who has to give you things beyond the second plane will come to your home by himself." So, I was sitting there waiting for him to come because he who is the owner of all creation knows who is sitting in his remembrance, who is sitting and yearning for him and where he is sitting. Only he knows when the time has come for a dear one to meet the Master. Supreme Father Kirpal himself sent one of his dear ones who came and told me, "Master wishes to come to your home today." I was very pleased to hear that the Master was coming. I said, "Master?" He replied, "Yes, Master is coming to your home today." You can just imagine that whatever that great power Baba Sawan Singh had said, was that not true? He had said, "The Master will come to your home by himself," and that came true. God sees everyone; Master sees everyone. He was seeing, that is why he himself met with the person who was sitting in his remembrance for eighteen years and was yearning for him.

This cup of love belongs to our owner, to our Lord. Whenever he wants, and to whomever he wants, he gives it. He fills the cup of those with whom he is pleased. The Mahatma whom God likes and for whom God has made the decision: "Whatever I give him, and whatever he gives to the person within whom he will put the Naam, I will liberate that soul." All those things are kept in the hands of God himself.

---

[3] The Five Words refers, on the outer level, to the mantra given by the Masters at initiation. They focus the soul's attention and function as passwords to the five planes. On the inner level, it refers to the manifestations of the inner Sound Current originating from the five different inner planes that the soul hears and merges with during its inward ascent. The Two Words refers to the first two of the Five Words given at initiation and provide passage through the first two planes but not beyond and refer to the manifestation of the inner Sound Current originating from the first two inner planes.

The Disease of Yearning

O Farid, I saw the eyes that once attracted the world.
The eyes which once could not bear coarse mascara are now the nest of birds.

Once Farid Sahib was passing by a graveyard and he saw a dead body which had been taken out from a grave by dogs or some other animals. The flesh of that body was eaten up by insects and in the cavity where the eyes had been, some creatures had made nests where they laid their eggs. Looking at the pitiful condition of that dead body, Farid Sahib said, "I saw those eyes that once attracted the world."

You know that through our eyes we attract people; the husband attracts his wife, and the wife attracts her husband. You know how we fascinate people through our eyes. "Some people are killed by the eyes; some people are liberated by the eyes. Within these eyes there is poison, within these eyes there is nectar. O Blind of Intellect, just look, because Satguru has given you eyes."[4] There is everything in the eyes.

Here he says, "I have seen those eyes that once attracted the attention of the whole world. The eyes which could not even bear the coarse lampblack have now become a nest for creatures." Women here in India have the habit of putting lampblack [mascara] on their eyes. If it is not ground well, if it is coarse, they do not like it, because if you put coarse lampblack on your eyes then you can feel it and it can be painful. He says the eyes that would not even bear coarse lampblack have now become the home of those creatures. Those creatures have made nests, they have laid eggs, and they have raised their children there. Feeling sorry for that soul, he said, "O Dear One, if, after getting this human body, you had done the devotion of and had realized God Almighty, then your body would not suffer so much and you would not have wasted your human birth."

O Farid, Saints give the advice, shouting, calling every day.
But those who have chosen the devil, how can they turn away from him?

---

[4] Sant Ji is quoting his hymn, "O Akal Ke"; see *Songs of the Masters 2002*, p 31.

The Pain of Separation

Farid Sahib lovingly says, "God Almighty has always been sending Saints and Mahatmas, his beloved children, into this world and through the satsang they tell people, shouting aloud, 'Protect yourselves, save yourselves; you are being swept away in this ocean of the world; you are losing your life.'" There is nothing in this world which will go with you. You know that when a wife leaves her body, her husband goes on crying and can do nothing more than that. The wife leaves him. In the same way, when a husband leaves his body, his wife can do nothing but cry, and bemoan his death. The parents keep sitting and the children leave and the parents cannot do anything for them. There is no one who can help us at that time.

Mahatmas ask us, "Who is there in this world who can be called your own and who can help you?" Guru Teg Bahadur Ji says, "I have seen false love in this world. Everyone loves others because of his own selfish motives. Whether he is brother or friend, son or wife, they all love for their own interests." Everyone says, "Mine, mine," but they do that only because of their own interest. This foolish mind has not yet understood this. Nanak says, "You will be able to cross this ocean of life only if you do *bhajan*[5] and simran and do the devotion of God." That is why lovingly Farid Sahib says that Saints and Mahatmas come into this world and they tell us again and again which things are our very own and which things do not belong to us. They tell us who can help us and who cannot. Every day they give us teachings and instructions.

Guru Ram Das Ji says, "O Saints, O Brothers, listen to what the Masters say. Stretching out their arms they are calling you to come back home." A ferryman on the bank of a river calls out to people that those who want to cross the river should come and sit in his boat. He assures them that he is experienced and knows how to take the ferry across the river. "Since I know everything about taking the ferry across and everything about the river, I will make you reach your destination safely." Just like that ferryman, Masters come to this world and shout aloud, "O Dear Ones, I have the grace of Almighty God, and with his grace and blessings I have been given

---

[5] The meditation practice of listening to the Sound Current. The term "bhajan" can also indicate spiritual verses or hymns generally meant to be sung.

The Disease of Yearning

this ship of Naam. If you believe in me and sit in this ship of Naam you will also get liberation; you will be able to cross this ocean of life." Further he says, "If you are seeking happiness and peace for your soul, then go to the Master and accept his shelter."

Farid Sahib says here that they shout aloud, and every day they give us wise advice. But how can those who are deluded by the wicked ones ever devote themselves to God Almighty? Some people have been deluded by the Negative Power. They say, "Why do we have to do the devotion of the Lord? It is for other people only. For us there are the worldly pleasures. What is the use of going to the Master now and getting Naam initiation? We may do it later on because the Masters never refuse. Whenever we want, we can go and get Naam initiation." So here Farid Sahib says that those who have been deluded by the Negative Power, by that wicked one, how can they ever come to the path of devotion and do bhajan and simran? Such people go on making plans but death waits for no one. At the appropriate time death comes and she catches hold of those people. He says that such people's minds have been deluded by that wicked one and no matter how much you explain to them, they can never come to the path of devotion.

Guru Nanak Dev Ji Maharaj says that no matter how much you explain to the manmukh, still he will go astray. He says that no matter how much you try to lead the manmukh on the right path, still he will always go astray. It means that his path will always be different from the path of the *gurumukh*.[6] Mahatmas lovingly say that gurumukhs and manmukhs cannot get along with each other because they both have their own different path. As oil and water cannot mix with each other, in the same way gurumukhs and manmukhs cannot mix with each other. One liberates you and the other drowns you.

He says that gurumukhs and manmukhs are like two sons of the same father going to school. One passes the examination and one fails. One of them studies wholeheartedly, gets a good education and becomes an

---

[6] Literally "mouthpiece of the Guru", a highly advanced or perfect disciple, the opposite of a manmukh.

The Pain of Separation

officer while the other does not study hard and he does not get any degree. He ends up taking care of animals and doing other jobs like that. This is a unique play created by God Almighty. That is why he says that gurumukhs and manmukhs cannot get along with each other.

Why can't gurumukhs and manmukhs get along with each other? Because gurumukhs are those who enjoy the meditation of Shabd Naam, and manmukhs do not care for meditation. Gurumukhs always understand that manmukhs are only collecting the skins of the fruit. They consider outer rites and rituals to be like collecting the skins, shells, and peels of fruit, whereas doing the meditation of Shabd Naam is like eating the fruit. Those Beloveds of God always try to withdraw our attention from the outer casing; they want our attention to go to the fruit within. Swami Ji Maharaj also says, "You can't get anything by churning water; it is a pity that you are too lazy to churn milk." We know that no matter how much we churn water we can never get any butter from it; we will get only foam. We obtain butter only after churning milk. It means that we are too lazy to do the meditation of Shabd Naam; we are too lazy to do the devotion of God. Guru Nanak Sahib also says, "Man gets up to do bad things but when the time comes for doing meditation he sleeps." Farid Sahib says that no matter how much you explain to one who has been deluded by the Negative Power still he will refuse and he will not accept the teachings of the Master.

> *O Farid, become like grass*
> *If you want to realize the Lord.*
> *First it is cut, then crushed under foot;*
> *Then it is made to enter the door of the Lord.*

Someone once came and asked Farid Sahib, "How can one realize God and get the honor of entering the kingdom of God?" Here, in a very beautiful example, he is explaining to that dear one, "O Dear One, if you want to realize God, make your mind like grass. You know that someone walks on grass, someone curses that grass and someone twists and rolls it into a rope. But grass does not call anyone bad. It does not think ill of others;

The Disease of Yearning

it loves everyone." From grass we make ropes, and from ropes we make prayer mats which we use in the satsangs. When dear ones sit on those mats and meditate on Naam, that grass also gets liberation. So here he says, "O Dear One, if you want to realize God you will have to make your mind like that grass; you will have to bear everything and tolerate everything. In that way you will get liberation and you will be able to enter the kingdom of God."

He says if you want to do the devotion of God you have to fulfill certain conditions. What are those conditions? First of all, you have to give up worry about public shame. You have to give up pride of your worldly position and bear taunts and criticisms. Tulsi Sahib says, "O Tulsi, to fight in the battlefield is the work of a moment or two, but the fight with the mind goes on every day and we have to fight without any sword." He says that fighting in the battlefield is decided in a moment or two; you either kill or get killed. But the battle which we fight with our mind goes on every day and in this fight we have no weapon to use, we fight empty-handed. What weapon do we have in this battle? The only weapon we have is the weapon of Shabd, the weapon of the Sound Current with which our Satguru has armed us.

Guru Nanak says that no matter if we have to fight with five strong beings, still we have the mighty hand of the Master on our back. The seat of our mind and soul is at the eye center, and the residence of the five passions, of lust, anger, greed, attachment and egoism, is also at the eye center. The astral residence of all these passions is in Trikuti. He says you are not alone in fighting these five strong passions, you have the support of your Master. He has armed you with the weapon of Shabd and his hand is on your back. Go within and see how your Master is helping you in this battle. Whatever you need, he provides you with it. Go within and see that your Master is present even before you reach there. Farid Sahib says if you want to go to the court of the Lord within, you must create love for him, and have humility and meekness.

> *O Farid, do not even criticize the dust, as there is nothing equal to dust.*
> *While living it is under your feet; after death it is upon you.*

The Pain of Separation

I have often said that only he who has some greed and desire will criticize others. Mahatmas who have meditated, and who have become perfect, shower grace even on those who are greedy and who criticize them. They always pray, "Almighty Lord, shower grace on them so that they will not spoil their human birth." They always save their disciples from this disease of criticizing others. Master Sawan Singh Ji used to say, "We get some kind of pleasure or taste from all the sense organs but when we use the tongue for criticism, it does not have any taste. It is neither sour nor sweet." It does not have any taste, but still everyone is attached to it and everyone is being bothered by it.

Once someone criticized Farid Sahib and asked the people, "Why are you coming here? What does he have to offer?" Farid Sahib, after listening to the criticism, did not respond with criticism. He said lovingly, "O Dear One, you should never even criticize dust, because even dust can be very powerful. When a person is alive, dust may be under his feet, but when he leaves the body that dust gets on top of the human being." You know that in the grave, dust and sand cover the human body, so he says you should even be afraid of dust. He says if someone is making a mistake, don't pay any attention to it. God Almighty is there to punish the guilty ones and to reward the good ones. He sees everything.

O Farid, where there is greed there is no love. If there is greed the love is false. How can we pass even a day if the roof has a leak in it?

Once there was a person who imitated Farid Sahib. He would close his eyes and sit in meditation, and in order to attract people, he would do everything like Farid Sahib. He would try to attract rich people and make them his disciples, so that he could get more maya, because in fact he was the worshipper of maya. When a rich person came to him, he would tell them it was difficult to maintain the langar and they should contribute to it. He would say there was no good housing for the sangat and they should help make a house. He went on craving for maya and worldly things but outwardly he showed people that he was a mahatma.

Looking at his condition, Farid Sahib lovingly told him, "O Dear One, outwardly you close your eyes, sit in meditation, and show people that you

The Disease of Yearning

are a devotee of God. Like a crane standing on one leg, you do the devotion of the Lord, but within you are craving for maya." How is that possible? How can you love God and also love maya at the same time? How can two swords live in one case? He said you can do only one thing; either you can get God's love or you can fulfill the lust of your heart.

That is why he says, "Suppose it is raining and you are sitting in a broken hut. How long can you sit there? You will have to find some permanent place." He says you have the sickness of pleasures and passions, because whatever kind of food you eat you have its effect. You do not earn your own livelihood. You eat from other people's earnings; that is why you have this sickness. Outwardly you have the human body, but it is no more than a skeleton, because within you all those passions have plundered and have made you hollow.

Guru Nanak Sahib says that as an acid dissolves gold, in the same way lust and anger dissolve our bodies. He says, "You have already become old. How long will you sit in this body pretending to do the devotion of God, while in your heart you are desiring worldly pleasures? How long can you continue doing both these things? How long can you deceive people like this?"

So, giving practical examples which we come across in our day-to-day lives, Farid Sahib lovingly explains to us that we should also make our life sincere. We should do whatever work we have been given by the Master with all sincerity and honesty so that our Master's work may become easier. Kabir Sahib said, "O Benefactor, gracious on the poor ones, seeking your support, I have made all my family sit in your boat. Now, if it is in your Will, you may take the whole family across." After putting the souls in this ship of Naam, Mahatmas sail it across this ocean of life, with the support of God Almighty. They say, "O Lord, we have sailed this ship on the ocean of life with your support, now it is up to you. Only you know what you must do. If you wish, you can make the souls meditate; if you wish you can take them without making them meditate. We have left everything in your hands and now it is up to you. You have to protect all the souls."

When we give up the support of the world and seek only the support of our Master, he becomes worried for us. He also sees who has

The Pain of Separation

surrendered everything to him and he provides us with everything, he protects us. Master Sawan Singh Ji used to say, "If we become like a child, and if the Master gets upset and rebukes us, we feel it is very sweet and if he praises us, we think it is all the glory of the Master." It is very easy to say that we make our mind like a child, but very difficult to do it. When the Master rebukes us, we say, "Why did Master rebuke me?" and we get upset. Who likes the rebukes of the Master? Who feels that it is love that we are getting in the rebuke? Only those who really love the Master. Only those who see their own faults. They like the rebukes of the Master because they realize that it is their own fault that they are getting rebuked. They say, "If the Master forgives me, if the Master glorifies me and praises me, it is all his glory. O Lord, if people praise me it is all your glory and if they criticize me, still I will not leave you. If people praise us and say, 'He is a good person,' we would glorify you, we would understand that it is all your glory. Because we were not capable of doing anything; we were not the good ones. It is all your grace, all your glory, that you have made us become good. If people criticize us, even then we will not leave you. Because we have got the disease of yearning, the disease of the pain of separation from you, and the disease of singing your praise. We are not going to give up this disease no matter what people do to us."

Like an addict lives on his addiction, in the same way, devotees of the Lord live on the remembrance of God. If an addict does not get the thing to which he is addicted, he feels like his whole body is in pain and that he is going to die. When he gets the thing to which he is addicted, then he feels that his life has come back. In the same way, when those who are devoted to the Lord are able to do his devotion, they feel alive, but when they are not able to do the devotion of the Lord, when they are not able to connect themselves to God Almighty, with the Master, they feel that they have died. The devotees of the Lord feel that the breath in which they did not remember God Almighty was an illegal breath; they should not have taken that breath.

Guru Nanak even says, "O Lord, if I forget you even for a moment, I feel as if I have forgotten you for fifty years." So, like Farid said, we should also develop that kind of love and yearning for our Master. Whether we

The Disease of Yearning

are sitting or standing, sleeping or awake, we should always remember the Master. We should go within and do his devotion because if we do his devotion, if we remember him all the time, he will open his door for us, embrace us, and make us sit in his lap. According to what Farid Sahib has told us, we should also take advantage of this valuable time, and make our birth successful.

Chapter 3

The Pain of Separation

In the last two satsangs I have said that all this garden is being looked after by Supreme Father Baba Sawan Singh Ji Maharaj. He was born in a time when people had given up the path of Naam. They had forgotten the teachings, the writings, the banis of the great Saints and Mahatmas. They had forgotten him so much, that they started searching for that conscious being, Almighty Lord, in stones, idols and water. They forgot where God is and how one can meet him. Sawan came into this world like rain comes in the month of Sawan; Sawan is the month of the Indian calendar which is near June and July. He came in the month of Sawan, which is very important to people who live in areas where there is little rain and where there are no good means of irrigation. Rain is their only source of water.

Similarly, for those souls who were yearning for God Almighty, those who were thirsty for him, Sawan came just as that rain comes in the month of Sawan to quench the thirst of the earth. God Almighty assumed the body of Baba Sawan Singh for those thirsty souls who were yearning to meet him. After coming into this world, Baba Sawan Singh showed the real path to those who had forgotten the path of devotion. He embraced those who, after worshipping stones and idols, had become like stone, and he showed them the real path. He told them the truth, that we cannot realize God from anywhere outside. He is within us; he is hungry for our love. Baba Sawan Singh lovingly explained to them that God Almighty is for

The Pain of Separation

all, he is not the personal property of any one religion or community. He is one for all and everyone has an equal right to meet him. God Almighty does not belong only to America and not to India; God is not only for Americans and not for Indians. No, he is for everyone. He is for all those who remember him and do his devotion.

Master Kirpal Singh Ji used to say that it is the law of nature that there is food for the hungry and water for the thirsty. Nature always provides us with the things we need. For those souls who had the yearning and the pain of separation from him, God Almighty assumed the form of Baba Sawan Singh and came into this world. He loved them and he showed them the real path.

In those days there were many people, many hot-tempered people, who used to go to Baba Sawan Singh and talk about their own rites and rituals. They would always debate with him, and they always tried to prove that their rites and rituals were the best and were the only successful practices. Baba Sawan Singh Ji would say, "Yes, I agree, what you say is correct, what you say is true. But I would advise you to go within and see reality with your own eyes." When people would play musical instruments to do devotion and say, "This is the only way of doing the devotion of the Lord," Baba Sawan Singh Ji would say, "Yes, now you have come to awaken God Almighty." He also used to say, "Guru Arjan Dev compiled the Guru Granth Sahib and in that he also included the bani of Kabir which says, 'O Mullah, why do you climb the minaret of the mosque and shout so loud? The Lord is not deaf.' He is aware of your thoughts even before you think them."

You know that when we are going to do any good deed, give a donation, etc., we do it in a place where there are many other people, so that they may see that we are doing a good deed. We even go to pundits and astrologers to find out which day is auspicious for doing that good deed. But when doing bad deeds or sins, we do not even consult our parents. A husband does not consult his wife nor vice versa; whoever gets the opportunity, and whenever they want to, they do that sin without letting anyone know that they are committing a sin. Now you see that even though we sit inside and hide it from other people when we do bad deeds, still the

The Pain of Separation

consequences of those bad deeds are manifested outside, and we are paying for those bad deeds now. How are we paying for those bad deeds? You know that all the worldly difficulties we have, the problems of unemployment, difficulties at home, and other difficulties, they are all like punishment for our past bad deeds. Whatever little bit of good deeds we have done, we are also getting the rewards for that. What are the rewards? The rewards are that we have good health, we have good intellect, our children obey us, we have a comfortable means of earning a livelihood.

Mahatmas lovingly explain to us that God Almighty, sitting within us, sees every action of ours. People have left no stone unturned in searching for God. They have tried so many different ways of doing the devotion of the Lord. If by coloring our clothes or by adopting any particular kind of dress one could realize God, then that would be the cheapest bargain. It doesn't take much to color our clothes or to adopt an outer appearance. But he cannot be pleased with all that. All those things only attract the people of the world. We cannot please God Almighty by changing our clothes or disguising ourselves with a different form of dress. If we could realize God just by doing that, then those actors who always go on changing their outfits would have realized him easily. But those people are still in this world working hard for their livelihood.

Usually, we people have the belief that if we go on a pilgrimage and bathe in certain places, we will get liberation and realize God. But Kabir Sahib says, "If just by bathing in holy waters one could realize God, then frogs, fishes and other creatures in the water would have realized God Almighty long ago; they would have been liberated from those suffering bodies." But that is not true; they are still there and they are suffering in those bodies.

If God could be realized only by giving away donations, then only rich people would have realized him. If God Almighty could be realized only by reading and writing, then those dear ones who go on reading and writing day and night would have realized him. Only the clever ones would have realized him; innocent or uneducated people would never have gotten the opportunity to realize him.

That is why Mahatmas lovingly explain to us that the path by which we can meet him, the practices which we can do to realize him, are created

The Pain of Separation

by God himself. He has done it according to his own wishes and he himself has put it within all of us. No one can increase that path, no one can decrease that path. Guru Nanak Dev Ji Maharaj says, "He who owns this house has locked it himself; we can get the key from the Master." No matter how many things you do, how much effort you make, without going into the refuge of the Master, you cannot enter this house. God always sends Saints with the key which opens the lock which he himself has put in this human body. Sometimes that key was in the hands of Guru Nanak; sometimes Kabir; sometimes Baba Sawan Singh. Whenever God wants, and to whomever he wants, he gives the key. He always gives it to the Mahatma of the present time. No matter how many efforts you make using your mind and intellect, you can never realize him. He can be realized only after going in the refuge of the Master who has the key to open that lock.

Often, I have told how in my early days I got the opportunity to do different kinds of outer rites and rituals. I used to perform austerities and do *jaldhara,* a practice in which a flow of water falls on the center of one's head. Usually it is done in the winter months and the water is very cold. The person who is doing that practice repeats some kind of mantra of the name of the Lord. I got the opportunity to do all those rites and rituals, but I did not get any contentment or any peace of mind. Until I went to the Masters and bowed at their feet, I did not get any peace. So that is why he lovingly says that no matter how many good deeds you do, still you cannot realize him. Kabir Sahib says, "Just as there is oil in the sesame seed, and fire in the stone, in the same way, O Dear One, your Beloved resides within you. If you can wake him up, you may do so."

Just as there is fire in the stone, oil in the seeds, fragrance in the flowers, color in the leaves, and *ghee* (clarified butter) in the milk, in the same way, God resides within you. That is why all Saints agree that this human body is the real temple, entering which we can realize God.

If we are not searching within this human body, but are going outside, to the outer temples and holy places which we have made with our own hands, to search for God, we cannot get anything but difficulties. We should try to understand why Saints made those holy places like temples

The Pain of Separation

and mosques. Those places of worship were made to tell us that we should take good care of them; we should not take any meat, wine or any dirty thing there. This was just to inspire us to go within, because whatever is within, that is also outside.

If we think about the rites and rituals which people do in different religions, we will see that they are all similar and they have the same message to give. When we enter a Hindu temple there are bells. After hearing them we see a light burning and bow our head to that light. In the same way if we go to a mosque, there also they burn a light and the priest shouts aloud and calls the name of God. If we go to the temples of the Sikhs, there we see musical instruments and they blow a conch and beat a drum; they also have a constant flame of light. In Christian churches they have a big bell which they ring before the service and before they start the prayers, they also burn candles. In this way, the practices of all religions are similar and the purpose of doing all these outer rites and rituals is to search for God. But we forget. We take very good care of the outer temples and mosques; we keep them very clean and do not even wear our shoes when entering temples. But this temple of God, this human body which God Almighty himself has made, did we ever take care of it? Did we ever appreciate it? Did we ever enter into it? If someone breaks down or destroys an outer temple which we have made, in order to avenge that action, we destroy thousands of real temples which God has made. After all those killings, we call ourselves martyrs, representatives of the religion. Man loves the temples of bricks and stone which he has made, but he does not love the temple which God has created. He hates the temple made by God.

In his bani Farid Sahib will tell us, "O Dear One, if you are fond of realizing God, if you want to meet God, don't hurt anyone's feelings because there is no sin which can be greater than the sin of hurting the feelings of others." Every day I have been commenting on Sheikh Farid's bani. Farid Sahib had wandered very much in the forest performing austerities in search for God, but when he met the perfect Master, after that he sat down at one place and did his meditation.

One person called Shah Saraf also used to wander from forest to forest searching for God. Sometimes he went to the same forest in which Sheikh

The Pain of Separation

Farid did the devotion of God. Many times, he met with Sheikh Farid and they had very loving talks. Farid Sahib once told him, "O Sheikh Saraf, why are you wandering here and there in the forest; why are you stepping over bushes and thorns? God Almighty, for whom you are searching, is nowhere outside; he is within your own heart. Why are you searching for him outside?"

> *O Farid, why wander from forest to forest, stepping on the thorns and stones?*
> *God resides within; why search for him in the forests?*
>
> *O Farid, with my tiny legs I traversed the plains and mountains.*
> *Today, Farid, even the pot seems to be thousands of miles away.*

Only those who have searched for God know how they have to struggle with the mind in order to do the devotion of the Lord. Only they know how they have to eat less, sleep less, drink less and how they have to bear all the sufferings of their bodies. You know the price which we have to pay for achieving happiness is pain. A mother cannot give birth to a child without experiencing pain. If we want to have gold, we have to go into a gold mine and work hard to get it out from there. If we want to have a pearl, we have to dive into the depths of the ocean. In the same way, in the path of spirituality, the work of realizing God, one has to sacrifice a lot, one has to work very hard.

Farid Sahib suffered a great amount of hunger and thirst, because he did a lot of meditation. You know that when we eat too much, we fall asleep, we become lazy. To avoid sleep, meditators always eat little; that is why their bodies are not as strong as the bodies of those who eat a lot. You know that we people eat too much, we have become fat. We eat too much; we sleep too much. When Farid Sahib became old his body was weak because he had done so much meditation and he had suffered so much hunger and thirst. Lovingly he says, "Using these legs I have traveled so much…." You know in those days there were no good means of transportation like trains, jeeps and cars; people did their traveling on foot. That is why Farid Sahib says, "There was a time when I walked to so many

The Pain of Separation

different places, but now I have become so old that I cannot even sit in meditation because my body has become very weak." Since he became sick also, he says, "The pot which is put near my bed, even that seems to be far away from me." It is not far away, but because of sickness and old age it seems to be very far beyond reach. So here he is describing his condition, his old age.

O Farid, the nights are long and my sides ache.
Curse on their lives, who prolong their hopes.

Now he says that in the Golden Age, Silver Age and Copper Age[1] we lived long lives and slept for many long nights. Sleeping long nights means that we lived long lives. Even our body gets tired by sleeping too much. He says, "Curse on those who are still drowning in this ocean of life, those who did not do the devotion of God, even when they were given such a long life, those who did not realize God, and those who are still wandering here and there in this world. Curse on their lives because they did not take advantage of the birth they were given." That is why he asks, "What is the life of those who have to come back into this world again and again?"

Our condition is not different from theirs, because after every death we are taken to the Lord of Judgment. He looks at the paper on which our accounts are written, and according to our deeds, he sends us to the place where we belong. He sends us into different bodies, and to different places where we will suffer the consequences of the bad deeds which we did in our earlier life. Before we enter another body, we have to face death from this body. What is our condition? We come back into this world again and again; we are born in this world and we leave this world. Lovingly he asks: What is the life of those people who have to come back into this world

---

[1] Along with the Iron Age, these ages make up the four ages or *yugas* in one cosmic cycle, according to Hindu cosmology. Human life span in the Golden Age is believed to be 100,000 years, in the Silver age 10,000 years, in the Copper Age 1,000 years and in the Iron Age 100 years.

The Pain of Separation

which is not their own, again and again, this world where you do not have anyone of your own, you do not have anyone who can help you?

O Farid, if I had kept anything hidden from you,
O My Incoming Friend, may my flesh be put on coals and made red.

One old man whose name was Jassa Lohar used to come to the forest where Sheikh Farid meditated. He came there to collect firewood, then he would sell it; in that way he made his living. Once when he came to the forest collecting wood, it became very late, and since he was an old person too, he thought, "Why not stay with Farid through the night, and tomorrow I will collect some more wood, and then I will go back." He thought, "Just as I always cook some food every night, Farid also may be preparing food, and when it is ready, he will tell me, 'Come Dear One, let us have dinner.'" He waited and waited, but Farid Sahib loved his meditation, and did not come out of meditation and did not make any food to eat. In the middle of the night, it became too much for Jassa to bear, so he asked Farid Sahib, "Farid, give me some food to eat." Farid Sahib laughed and lovingly told him, "Look here, O Dear One, if I had any food with me, I would definitely have given it to you. I am telling you the truth; if you think that I am lying, may my whole body burn in the fire. But I am telling you the truth; I do not have any food to offer you, because even I am living on the support of God."

When Master Sawan Singh Ji went on tour, usually he would carry food for the whole day with him. He never liked to go to hotels, nor did Supreme Father Master Kirpal go to hotels; he also would carry food for the whole day with him whenever he traveled. Once Master Sawan Singh went out with one of his dear ones, taking food with him. The dear one who was accompanying Sawan Singh thought, "Maybe Master will ask about the food, or maybe the other dear one who is accompanying us will ask for some food." But Master Sawan Singh Ji did not ask, so they did not eat food on that day. When they came back in the evening Master Sawan Singh Ji said, "Look here, O Dear One, if the Masters were living in the physical bodies only then would they feel hungry and thirsty. You should

The Pain of Separation

know that Master gets some other food from within; there is some other power, something else, which keeps the Master satisfied and content. They get food from within." When they come into their physical body only then do they feel hungry and thirsty, but when they are not in their physical body they do not feel any hunger or thirst.

That is why Farid lovingly tells that dear one, Jassa, "I am sitting here in this forest having the support of God Almighty, and I am here only to do the devotion, only to meditate. If I had to eat and sleep then I could have easily done that living with my family. What was the use of coming into the forest if I would still go on eating and sleeping?"

The farmer wishes to eat grapes but plants a thorny bush.
He spins the wool but wishes to wear silk.

Now Farid Sahib says, "Is this justice, that the farmer is sowing the seeds of thorny bushes, but is expecting to enjoy grapes? He is weaving inferior quality wool, but he expects the shawl to be very soft." How is that possible? Mahatmas lovingly tell us: O Man, you are sowing inferior seeds which produce bitter fruits, but you expect to enjoy delicious fruits. You are sowing seed from bitter fruit but you expect to eat mangoes. How is that possible? Dear one, whatever you sow, you will have to harvest that.

Guru Nanak Sahib also says that in this field of the human body, whatever you sow, in the end you must harvest that. You yourself have to suffer the consequences of the karmas you are doing. In this world, he who has sown seeds of the chili will get only chilies from that plant; he who has planted sugar cane will harvest sugar cane. It is not possible for the person to harvest sugar cane if he has sown chilies. So that is why Mahatma Farid Sahib Ji lovingly explains to us, "What kind of justice is this if we sow one thing and expect something else?" Many dear ones come to me and they request me to open the veil for them; they request me to take them within. I tell them to purify their life, to meditate. They reply, "No Master, we cannot do that." So how is it possible to remove the veil and go within if we do not want to purify our lives and meditate? Can anyone open the veil without working for it? Can anyone get inner vision just by sleeping?

The Pain of Separation

If the farmer does not work hard and if he goes on sleeping all the time, do you think that he will be able to harvest anything from his field? In the same way, if any businessman says that he will not go out to buy things nor set up shop to sell those things, how is he going to make any money? We should understand that this is the special grace of God Almighty that we have been given Naam initiation. We do not have to pay any price for it; we have been given it without any charge. The only thing we must do is get up early in the morning, meditate for a couple of hours, and make our lives pure. If we are not ready to do even that, then how can God Almighty, how can our Master, lift the veil for us?

Once some disciples came to Guru Amar Das Ji Maharaj and requested, "Master, shower grace on us." Guru Amar Das replied, "First of all, prepare yourself for the time of nectar." It means, first of all get up in the morning time, which is called the nectarful time, and meditate.

> *O Farid, the streets are muddy, the home of the Beloved is at a distance, but*
>   *I love my Beloved.*
> *If I go my blanket becomes wet; if I don't go my love breaks.*

Now Farid is very anxious to go within and meet his Master. He says, "The streets are dirty, but I am also in love with my Beloved. If I go now, I will become dirty, if I don't go my love with him will break." What are the streets which are dirty? The streets are lust, anger, greed, attachment and egoism. If the soul goes there, she gets the dirt of all those passions, and the intellect also becomes dirty and becomes very heavy because of the dirt of all those passions. He says, "If I go to meet my Beloved, I will get dirty, but if I don't go my love with him will break. The shawl which I am wearing has become very heavy with the burden of sins which I am carrying." Further he will tell us, "It doesn't matter if the shawl which I am wearing is full of sins, if it is dirty and heavy with bad karmas. I should go and meet my Beloved, because he in whose remembrance I am sitting, whose devotion I am doing, he is aware of my weakness and shortcomings. He knows what I am doing, and he himself will remove the dirt from my shawl; he himself will purify me." He says, "No matter

The Pain of Separation

what happens, I will go and meet my beloved Master who has given me Naam initiation."

In Sikh history it is written that if a tiger, after hearing the sound of a gun, turns in a different direction, it will not be considered brave. In the same way, if sesame is afraid of going into the oil mill, who will appreciate the oil, who will be able to put it on their head? Similarly, if someone, after receiving Naam initiation and becoming the disciple of a perfect Master, goes away from the Master and defames the path, who will call him a disciple? It is exactly the same as if a comb is afraid of the cuts used to make her. If she is afraid of that pain, how will she get the honor of being used on people's heads? So here he says that unless you sacrifice yourself in this path of God, you cannot realize him. He says, "No matter how dirty and heavy my shawl is, still I will go to my Master. I will meet him because he who has given me Naam initiation will remove all dirt, will purify me."

Let my blanket be soaked in the rains sent by God.
But I must meet my Beloved and not break my love.

O Farid, I had the pride of turban (of position).
My intellect became dirty. But my ignorant mind did not know that even my
  head would roll in dust.

Now he lovingly says, "Wearing white clothes and being proud of possessing a lot of wealth, we hesitate to do seva. We think that our clothes will get dirty, or that people will think badly of us if they see us feeding the poor." He says, "This was my misunderstanding. This body has been made of mud and one day this body must once again turn into mud. My forgetful mind, my forgetful being, did not realize that one day I have to go and return to mud." We can take advantage of this body only by removing the egoism and by doing seva and simran as much as possible. Master Sawan Singh Ji used to say, "When both the poor and rich sit together on the same mat and eat together, the poor get inspiration and the rich get the opportunity to be humble." When both poor and rich do seva together, it inspires us to go within. The Master who has connected us with the Shabd

The Pain of Separation

Naam also becomes very pleased with us when he sees that his dear children have given up their egoism and pride and are working together.

> *O Farid, sugar candy, jaggery, honey and buffalo milk,*
> *All these things are sweet. But none is equal to God's sweetness.*

Farid Sahib meditated all his life long. Now he is telling us, people who run after tastes, that no doubt sugar, honey, and all sweet things are sweet, but if you would connect yourself with that power of Naam, you will feel that it is the sweetest of all. The taste or the scent you get from the nectar of Naam cannot be found in any other thing.

> *O Farid, my bread is of wood; my appetizer is my hunger.*
> *Those who eat buttered bread will suffer a lot.*

He used to live in the forest and whenever hunger would bother him too much he would go into town and beg some food to eat. Once when he went to beg food, he was taunted by a woman who said, "Even after becoming a fakir you are begging? Don't you feel embarrassed doing this?" Farid Sahib replied, "I know it is not a good thing, but what can I do? I cannot control my hunger even though I have controlled the five passions: lust, anger, greed, attachment and egoism. I do not have any difficulty with them, but I cannot control my hunger; it bothers me a lot." Then that woman told Farid Sahib, "You are a renunciate and I am just a worldly person, but still I would like to give you some advice. I will give you an idea with which you can reduce your hunger." She told him that every day he should rub the cup in which he takes food so that its size would decrease. If he did it every day, he would not notice how he had reduced his hunger, and the day would come when he would control his hunger. Farid Sahib always used to rub the cup, and in that way the size of that cup went on decreasing, and one day he completely defeated his hunger, and after that he did not eat. Whenever he would feel hungry, he had a chapati which was made of wood, and just to give his mind a little satisfaction that he had eaten something, he would bite that chapati and, in that way, satisfy his hunger.

The Pain of Separation

Once a rich person invited Farid Sahib to come and have lunch with him. Farid lovingly replied, "Look here, O Dear One, now this chapati of wood is my food and hunger is the taste of it; those who are eating buttered chapatis and delicious food, in the end they will suffer a great deal." Then he said that the Beloveds of God always become grateful to Almighty God by eating just dry chapatis and whatever else they get. He said, "Looking at other people eating delicious food, you should not have the desire of eating the same kind of food. Whatever is written in your fate, you will get only that, and looking at other people's palaces and comforts, don't feel bad in your heart. Do the meditation of the Lord and accept his will."

Eating dry and unbuttered bread, drink cold water.
O Farid, do not tempt your mind by seeing the buttered bread of others.

Today I have not slept with my Beloved and my limbs ache.
Let me ask those unfortunate ones, "How do you pass your nights?"

In the beginning it is very difficult to bring your mind and attach it to the devotion of the Lord because in the beginning it does not get any interest in it and does not enjoy it. But it is the quality of the mind that once it starts liking something, afterwards it becomes very difficult to detach our mind from that thing. It is like when a child is born, whether it is a human child or the child of any other animal, at first he doesn't know that milk is coming out from the breast of his mother. He doesn't even know whether it is sweet or not; he has no interest in putting his mouth on the nipple and doesn't know how to get the milk. The mother has to teach him that. But once the child starts to get the milk and realizes how tasty it is, after that it becomes difficult for us to stop him from drinking milk. You would have seen that once a calf gets the taste of milk it doesn't want to stop. The owners do not want it to drink all the milk, but it is difficult to take it away from the cow. Sometimes they even have to tie the calf to keep it away from the cow. The condition of the meditator is the same. In the beginning it is difficult to enjoy meditation, but once

The Pain of Separation

he has tasted the fruit of meditation it becomes very difficult for him not to meditate.

People complain that they fall asleep in meditation. It is a very pitiful condition. In fact, this complaint is of those dear ones who have not yet gone within. Regarding his meditation, Guru Arjan says, "O Night, go on increasing, because I am in love with my Beloved. O Sleep, decrease, because I am attached to my Beloved." He says, "O Night, when you are finished, day will come; then I will have to meet people and do the things of the world. O Sleep, you are inviting pains and unhappiness; why don't you decrease? Let me remain attached to my Beloved." The meditator wishes that there would be one night six months long because he is in love with his Beloved. That is why he tells the night to increase and the sleep to decrease.

Farid Sahib says, "I did not meet my Beloved and my body seems to be breaking apart, and I feel pain all over my body." This is the condition of meditators. Further he says, "Let me go and ask those souls how they are able to live in this night of life, without meeting their Beloved even once."

Guru Nanak says, regarding meditation, that if the dear one forgets the Master even for a moment, he loses the love. He says if the disciple has forgotten doing the simran of the Master even for one moment, then it creates a gap between him and the Master. So here Farid Sahib says, "Let me go and ask those souls how they are able to spend the night of their life when they are not in union with the Beloved." Regarding meditation, Guru Nanak Sahib says, "Just as a person who is addicted to something feels that life is in that addiction, in the same way a meditator who is addicted to meditation feels that his life is in meditation." Just as an addict lives doing his addiction, in the same way lovers of God live doing meditation.

> *She who is neither cared for at her in-laws', nor does she have a place at her parents' home,*
> *And of whom even her husband takes no care, what kind of fortunate bride is she?*

Now he lovingly says that this world is like the in-laws' home for the soul, and Sach Khand, the place where the soul belongs, is like the parents'

The Pain of Separation

home. After getting separated from her parents, the bride has come into this home of her in-laws and she has become attached to them, just as our daughters, when they get married, leave our home and go to live with their in-laws and their husbands. No matter how much you tell them, they always prefer to spend the nights at their in-laws' home, and they don't like to go to their parents' home at all.

So here Farid Sahib says that their husband never talks to them, they do not enjoy the company of their husband, but still they say that they are married to him. Guru Nanak says, "I have neither enjoyed any company with my husband nor was I married to him. Only by talking about my husband, I feel myself as married to him. O My Beloved, I have never seen my Beloved; O My Dear One, I have never seen my beloved husband."

We people always say that we are married; we just talk about it and we feel that we are married to Almighty God. We say, "Yes, we have the Naam; we are connected with God." But we have never spent the night with him, we have never sat down and talked to him. Then how can we call or consider ourselves as married to him? That is why he talks about those people who have never seen God Almighty even in their dreams, but still they see themselves as representatives of their religion, and they say that they enjoy doing the devotion of God, even though they have never seen him. We have never even asked him, "Are you pleased with me or displeased with me?" We ourselves are in the deception and we also deceive others. We have spoiled our lives and we are spoiling others' lives also. That is why here Guru Sahib says, "Fortunate are those souls who have met the Master, because they are the only ones married to God Almighty."

> *She is free of in-laws and of her parents. Her heart is her Husband's, who is unreachable and infinite.*
> *Nanak says, she who gets the care-free God is the blessed one.*

This verse was written by Guru Nanak Dev Ji. He says that the soul who, even after coming to the in-laws' home, is still connected with God Almighty is the blessed one, and when she goes back to Sach Khand there also she is connected to him. She is always married; she is always

The Pain of Separation

the fortunate one and I am ready to kiss the feet of such a soul. The souls whom God Almighty likes, those whom he chooses, only they are brought to the Master. In fact, God Almighty inspires them himself, and gives them initiation and makes them meditate.

You may read the bani of Kabir Sahib and all the other Masters who have come into this world. They have all written the same thing; they say that only if we are very fortunate do we get the Master and Naam initiation. We can understand the teachings of the Master only if we are very fortunate. Unless we are fortunate, we cannot have the desire to get initiation. Guru Arjan says, "When past karmas begin to sprout, one meets a loving renunciate soul, the Master. Nanak says, then the darkness is removed, God is met, and one gets up from the slumber of birth after birth."

When we get the reward of the good karmas of our past lifetimes, only then does the meeting with a Saint take place. We understand and appreciate him only if we are fortunate. We take advantage of his grace only if God Almighty also is gracious on us. Until then we are sleeping. Now we may say that we are not sleeping, we are awake, but no, that is not true. Masters always say that at present you are sleeping towards God, although you may be awake towards the world. Our real home, Sach Khand, where we have to go and reside, does not get destroyed in the dissolution or grand dissolution. That is our permanent abode. We do not have any concern about our real home nor do we make any effort to go back to our real home, but we are worried for the homes we have made in this world, the homes which we have to leave one day. We are attached to them; we are in love with them, but we do not love Sach Khand which is our real home. Are we not sleeping in the sleep of misunderstanding?

> *She bathed and perfumed herself and slept without worries.*
> *O Farid, but the bad smell of asafetida remained; the fragrance of musk went away.*

God has showered grace on us, he has given us Naam initiation and he has showered so much grace on us that he has given us simran. Simran cleans us within and it finishes all our sins. As the broom sweeps away

The Pain of Separation

all the dirt from a room, in the same way simran cleans our soul. Here he says, "Before accepting me he did not ask whether I had taken a shower, whether I had applied makeup, or whether I looked beautiful or not. God Almighty did not look at any of those things. He only saw the love which I had for him. Looking at my love he gave me the reward of that love, and the reward was that he made me meet him. Now I am free from all kinds of worries and anxieties; I am sleeping at his door without any worries. It means that now I have taken my boat across this ocean of life and have reached my real home."

Which boats do not make it to the other shore? Which boats drown in the middle of the ocean? You know that if we put a little asafetida, something which has a bad smell, next to a very fragrant thing, the bad smell will take away the fragrance of that fragrant thing. In the same way, he says that those people who have ego within them, people who do not believe in the existence of God, and who do not do his devotion, they are drowned in this ocean of life, even though they are kept with the fragrant ones. Even though they keep the company of the good ones, still, because of their egoism, they do not take any advantage of them and they are drowned in this ocean of life.

Egoism is a wall which stands between us and God Almighty. Guru Nanak says that man comes in egoism, man goes in egoism, man eats in egoism, man loses in egoism, and man burns in egoism; he does everything in egoism. Further he says that if one understands egoism and removes it, only then can he realize Almighty God. When one becomes free of egoism, only then does he get real knowledge. Then he understands what egoism is, how it is created, and what the medicine is for removing egoism. Guru Nanak says that egoism is a severe disease, but the remedy to remove it is also within us. If God Almighty showers grace on us, and makes us earn the Shabd, only then can we remove this egoism. Without God, egoism is an incurable disease, because man does not know what egoism is and from where it is being created. It is a very sweet disease which eats a man up from inside. Guru Nanak says only if God Almighty showers his grace and makes one earn the Shabd can one remove egoism. He says, "O Lord, those upon whom you shower grace, make them do the

The Pain of Separation

meditation of Naam." As we go on meditating on Naam, we come closer to God Almighty. Often, I have said that the physical residence of the five passions, of lust, anger, greed, attachment and egoism, is at our eye center and the astral residence is in Trikuti. Unless we take our soul beyond Trikuti, we cannot become free of egoism. Unless we remove the physical, astral and causal covers from our soul, and reach Daswan Dwar which is in the third plane, beyond Trikuti, we cannot get rid of egoism completely. As long as we are within the limit of the mind, he will always attack us with one or another passion, and he will keep us involved in egoism.

> *If my youth goes, I do not fear, as long as I do not lose the love of the Lord.*
> *O Farid, many youths have dried up (like the leaves) without the love of the Lord.*

Now Farid Sahib says, "I am not afraid of old age. Now that I am getting older, I am afraid and worried for my love for the Master. I do not want my love for him to go away or break. Many people have come into this world and enjoyed their youth, their life, without the love of the Master. But those poor ones have dried up and, as the crop loses its life without water, in the same way those people who did not have love for the Master, they have lost their lives, they have dried up, without love for the Master."

> *O Farid, worry is my bed: sorrow is the rope; the pain of separation is the bedding.*
> *This is my life. O True Lord, you see this.*

Now, addressing God Almighty, Farid Sahib says, "O Lord, my bedding is made up of the worry which I have for your love, and the pain which I have had in my meditation is like the rope with which I have made my bed. My yearning is like the sheet I am using. This is my condition, O My Beloved. O My Dear One, at least look at my condition and see whether I am intoxicated in your love, or whether I am intoxicated in the love of the world. I understand the pains and discomforts which you give me as happiness and the most comfortable things."

The Pain of Separation

When Guru Gobind Singh was made to leave the fort of Anandpur Sahib and when, in his presence, two of his sons were buried alive in a wall that was being made, he did not complain. He remained happy in the will of God. In his writings at that time he said, "Tell the condition of the dear ones to the beloved Friend; without you, O My Beloved Lord, I am wearing a quilt made of difficulties, and my life is like living among snakes. For me, a poor bedding of the beloved Friend is much better than the good bedding and good luxuries of the butchers. I prefer to be in your company than to be in the company of the other people." Here, in the state of yearning, even though outwardly he was having many difficulties, still he said, "O Lord, I prefer to be here and have the bedding of thorns and bushes because here I have yearning for you; I am in love with you. It is much better than having thrones and good beds." That is why the Beloveds of God, whether they are given pains or happiness, do not decrease their love for the Master. Instead of decreasing their love during difficulties, they increase their love for him.

Everyone talks about bireh.[2] O Bireh, you are all in all.
O Farid, understand the body where the pain of separation is not created as the graveyard.

Now lovingly he talks about the pain of separation. He says that people talk about love but they do not understand it, nor what is meant by the pain of separation and yearning. They think that just by talking about the pain of separation and yearning they can achieve it. He says, "No, just talking about the pain of separation is not enough." He says, "O Bireh, you are like an emperor." Without having the pain of separation and without having yearning for the Master, we cannot even do the simran which we have been given by the Master himself. No one can do the seva of the Master unless he has the pain of separation and yearning for him.

---

[2] The deep pain of separation from the Lord.

The Pain of Separation

Farid Sahib says, "O Bireh, you are not the same as people think you are. If you ask me, in fact, you are the emperor of all." He says, "The body in which the pain of separation is not created, that body is like the dead body."

Guru Gobind Singh says, "What happens if you close both your eyes and, sitting in the meditation posture, contemplate something? Even if you have bathed in all seven oceans and visited all the places of pilgrimage, even if you have risen above this world and gone in the world beyond, I tell you the truth, only those who have loved have realized God." He says that there is no use sitting in samadhi like a crane if you do not have love within you because you do not know when your mind is going to wake you up from that samadhi, when he is going to disturb you in your so-called meditation. So that is why, first of all, he says that you need to develop love for him within you.

Once there was a Mahatma who used to meditate. He became perfect in his meditation. His inner vision got opened and his Master gave him darshan and asked him to ask for any boon and it would be granted. "If you want, I can make you king of the whole world. I will give you whatever you desire." But that Mahatma said, "No, Master, I don't want anything. Kindly give me the pain of separation from you, and give me yearning for you so that I may be able to do the meditation." He said, "Give me the pain of separation and yearning for you so that I may remember you; it does not matter if you do not meet me."

You see that those who know the pain of separation, those who have experienced the pain of separation, only they have appreciation for it. He who has experienced the pain of separation from his Beloved knows what the pain of separation is like. Only a sick person knows the value of being healthy. How can healthy people know what sickness is? Sawan had the pain of separation from his beloved Master. You know that he had so many followers but sometimes, sitting in the presence of so many dear ones, he would start weeping when he would remember the pain of separation from Baba Jaimal Singh. He would weep so much that many people would try to console him, but still he would not stop weeping. In the same way his beloved son, Master Kirpal, had the pain of separation

The Pain of Separation

whenever he would talk about his beloved Sawan Singh. Whenever the name of his Master would be mentioned, he would start weeping in his remembrance.

Those who have love for the Master, yearning for him, the pain of separation from him, without shedding tears, without showing other people that they are suffering the pain of separation, they are shedding tears inside. Within themselves they are remembering their Master. I have often said that there is no use weeping if we do not have our Master to console us; if you do not have someone who can wipe away your tears, what is the use of shedding tears? If we have manifested our Master within us, only then is it enjoyable to shed tears in his remembrance. Seeing other people weep in remembrance of Master, if we do the same, but we do not have the Master manifested within us, who can console us and give us courage? What is the use of shedding those outer tears? But if we are connected with God internally and have love and yearning for him, then Mahatmas say the tears we shed in that condition are more precious than the blood of martyrs. That is why Farid Sahib says, "My body is burning in the fire of yearning. There is only one remedy for this yearning, and that is the pain of separation, love of the Master."

Every day Farid Sahib has been lovingly explaining to us how we have to withdraw our attention from outside and go within if we want to meet our Beloved. He says we cannot finish this work by doing anything outside. We cannot solve our problem by going into the forests, or to the places of pilgrimage, or to temples or mosques. We will solve our problem and meet our Beloved when we go within. Guru Amar Das says that the temple of God is this human body in which the jewel of the knowledge of God is manifested. Your human body is the real temple of God. You will realize God only when you go within. So, we should also mold our lives according to the teachings of the Masters, purify our soul and go within so we can meet our Beloved there.

Chapter 4

God Will Call for Your Account

I have always said that this whole flower garden belongs to that omnipotent Sawan, he who was capable of doing everything. He always used to tell us his personal experiences; the lives of all Saints are filled with experiences. Guru Nanak said, "Who can derive benefit from the Saints? Only those who believe in the stories of the Saints and follow what they say, no matter if in doing so it appears that they may experience loss." Behind what they say, a lot is hidden. Everyone talks of spirituality but it not a matter of talking; it is a matter of meditation.

Sawan Ji Maharaj used to tell one story about an old woman whose daughter became sick. She always used to pray, "O Lord, I have seen everything of this world; may death come to me instead of my daughter." The Lord is sitting within every particle of this creation and he sees what the jivas are thinking. One day a cow came from outside and entered the old woman's house. The cow looked here and there. There was a pot on the fireplace whose bottom had become black from soot. While looking for something to eat, she got her head stuck in that pot. She became bewildered and started running around in the house. Since neither her face nor her horns were visible, and only the black bottom was visible, the old woman thought, "This may be the Angel of Death, whom I had been requesting to come. He has come to take me away instead of my daughter." She became afraid and said, "Look here, the girl is over there, I am just an

The Pain of Separation

old woman!" We jivas talk outwardly but do not live up to what we say and that is why we fail.

In Sialkot there used to live a Muslim fakir by the name of Hamza Gaus. He was a very accomplished ascetic and possessed many supernatural powers. There was a wealthy person who had everything but didn't have a child. We people give a lot of importance to having children in our lives. So, he and his family served that fakir a lot and when that fakir became pleased, he told them, "You will have four sons, but you will have to give one of them to me for the cause of spirituality." We people think, "What do Saints have with them? They only talk." But that is not true. Also, what happens also depends upon our faith. Anyways, after some time that wealthy person had four sons. They grew up but he did not give one of them to Hamza Gaus as promised. So, Hamza Gaus called him and told him, "Dear one, now you should give me one son as you had promised." For a year and half that wealthy person made excuses and hesitated in giving his son to that fakir. After that, one day he came to the fakir and said, "You know, I am a Hindu and you are a Muslim. If I give you my son, I will be humiliated in my community." When fakirs who have supernatural powers become displeased, at once they curse those who have upset them. So, since he was like that, Hamza Gaus made a vow saying, "This place is full of liars and those who don't keep their promises. I will not eat until this whole town is destroyed."

In the time of Guru Nanak Sahib there were many such fakirs, who possessed supernatural powers and used to curse people. Guru Nanak Sahib went to many such fakirs and put them on the right path. So along with Bhai Bala and Bhai Mardana, Guru Nanak Sahib went to Sialkot. Upon reaching there he told Hamza Gaus, "A fakir should have mercy in him. Why are you cursing these people?" He replied, "I will not eat until this whole town is destroyed." Guru Nanak Sahib said, "The people of this town have already accepted their death. How are you going to kill those who are already dead?" Hamza Gaus said, "How do I know that is true?" So, for his satisfaction, Guru Nanak Sahib sent Bhai Mardana with two coins of gold into the town with a request that he get the merchandise of "truth" and "falsehood." Bhai Mardana went to all the shops, but no one could give him such merchandise. After wandering through town, finally he came to a very good businessman, whose name was Mullah. Mullah took both coins and wrote on one piece of paper, "To live is false," and on the other paper he wrote, "To die is true." After taking those two papers, Bhai Mardana came to Guru Nanak Sahib, who showed them to Hamza Gaus and told him, "The people of this town are such that they believe to die is truth and to live is false. They have already accepted their death. How much more can you kill them?" In this way, Hamza Gaus was satisfied and he removed his curse from the people of that town.

Guru Nanak Sahib thought that this trader had written a very high thing. He wanted to see if he himself followed it or not. Guru Nanak Sahib went to his place and said, "I am ready to kiss your feet. Do you really live up to what you have written? Do you yourself believe in what you have written?" Mullah the trader replied, "I don't really believe in it. I wrote this only for the sake of money. But I would follow you, if you would make me understand it."

Mullah served Guru Nanak Sahib for some days and after that Guru Nanak Sahib became pleased with him. He told him, "I will make you my representative. You may give Naam initiation to those who desire it, and I will take care of those whom you initiate." But Mullah said, "Master, I cannot live without you. You have become everything to me." Guru Nanak Sahib replied, "No, you have your wife, your children. You should understand and take care of your responsibilities." Mullah said, "No Master, I know this for sure: I cannot live without you," and so he followed Guru Nanak.

One morning, after they reached the next destination, Guru Nanak told Mullah, "I have seen your wife getting ready to commit suicide as she feels that she was left alone. She had been encouraged by your enemies to sacrifice herself. If you wish you may go back to save her." At once Mullah's love for the Satguru disappeared and he said, "Please make me go back to her quickly because if she will die it will be a great loss. She means everything to me." After saying this he went back to his wife.

After some time, Guru Nanak also came back to Mullah's home and called for him. His wife came out and saw Guru Nanak, Bhai Bala and

The Pain of Separation

Bhai Mardana calling for Mullah. She told her husband that those three fakirs have come. Mullah asked his wife, "What do I do now? They will take me with them." His wife said to him, "Hide yourself in the dark room where we store the cow dung cakes (used as fireplace fuel), and I will tell them that you are not here, that you went with them and haven't returned since." When Guru Nanak Sahib kept calling Mullah, through the window his wife said to him, "He is not here. He went with you and since then he has not come back."

When the people in the neighborhood heard this, they got together and told Guru Nanak that they had seen Mullah at home just a little while ago. Guru Nanak Sahib then uttered this hymn; "Friendship with the Karyaras (the family name of Mullah) is false and falsehood is its foundation. O Mullah, you do not know the writ of fate, how your death will come."

Guru Nanak Sahib said, "O, Mullah you are playing tricks with me. You used to say that you cannot live without me even for a second, but you don't even know where you are going to die." In that room where Mullah was hiding, a snake came out and bit Mullah and he died. Everyone in that town came to know about that, about how Mullah, in order to avoid going with the Saint, hid himself in a dark room and died after being bitten by a snake. Guru Nanak Sahib knew the fate of Mullah was that he would have to go into many different bodies and live miserable lives. It was only through the company of the perfect Master that he could erase what was written in his fate. That is why he was calling Mullah to come and go with him.

After going into many different bodies, Mullah finally came in the body of a rabbit. This rabbit was killed by Guru Gobind Singh Ji in Nanded, when he went to the southern part of India and, in this way, Mullah was liberated. When a pious person, encouraged by his relatives, came to Guru Gobind Singh Ji for Naam initiation, he saw Guru Gobind Singh Ji feeding this rabbit to his falcon. He felt bad and said, "What kind of guru are you? You are killing animals and becoming happy?" Guru Gobind Singh Ji replied, "Dear one, you don't know the secret. This is a soul who was a companion of my great Master, Guru Nanak. Now his time had come so he is liberated." Why do such stories get known to people? Masters narrate such stories in the satsangs for the benefit of generations to come.

God Will Call for Your Account

In the same way, once Satguru Sawan Singh Ji Maharaj lovingly told a story from the times of Guru Gobind Singh Ji. He said once the congregation of the sangat and the Master was happening; satsang was going on and Guru Gobind Singh Ji was talking about discipleship. He said that disciples of the Master are rare; mostly people are the disciples of their wives, their children, their wealth and their possessions. Upon hearing this one follower got up and said, "No, Master, I am your disciple. I am not the disciple of my wife."

Guru Gobind Singh Ji tried to explain to him a few times that it was rare to find a disciple of the Master, but that dear one kept on insisting that he was the disciple of Guru Gobind Singh Ji and no one else was his master. So, Guru Gobind Singh Ji told him, "Okay, get me a roll of cloth which is unique and is such that there is no other roll like it available in the market." The follower went to the marketplace and bought a unique kind of cloth and brought it to his home. His wife saw it and asked him, "For whom did you buy this?" He replied, "For the Master." She said, "But I like this cloth and I want it." He replied, "But I got this for the Master and there is no other roll of cloth like this available." She said, "I don't care. You go and tell Guru Sahib that you searched but couldn't find a unique piece of cloth." He replied, "Dear one, how can I do that? He is all conscious. He knows everything." She said, "That is not my concern. I like this cloth and won't give it up." So, he gave that roll of cloth to his wife. Later when he went to the Master, because he loved going to satsang, the Master asked, "Yes, dear disciple, did you bring that cloth?" He started making excuses to the Master; "Well, Master, I am searching for it. I have not found it yet. I will keep looking and will get it soon," and so on. His wife had also followed him to satsang with that roll of cloth hidden in her dress. She took out that roll of cloth and presented it to the Master saying, "Master, he is not your disciple. He is my disciple."

Shringi Rishi was born in the forest and lived all his life in the forest. He never went to the towns. But when he had to fight with his mind, when a little spark of lust arose within him, he fathered not one or two, but thirteen children. Masters lovingly tell us that in everyone's life such incidents take place. Our Pathi Ji, who is sitting here, always used to praise

The Pain of Separation

one of his dear brothers, saying, "I have so many shortcomings, but my brother is very strong-willed and full of determination. However, he didn't get an opportunity to do devotion." That dear one is also sitting here and I have known him for the last twenty-five or twenty-six years. When Pathi Ji would praise his brother, I felt that beloved Kirpal within me should put him on the path and he should be given an opportunity to do devotion. Finally, he got initiation and, after that, for thirteen years he bothered me with his desire to live with me. He would say, "I can't live without you." I told him he could do that after he fulfilled his worldly responsibilities. With my beloved Master's grace his children got married and he became free from the responsibility of taking care of them, so he came to live with me. His family and his wife came with him to leave him at the ashram. Once he was at the ashram, though, his wife looked at him with such loving and charismatic eyes, like Shringi Rishi was shown by the woman who had gone to the forest to bring him to the town. Even great sages like Parashur were made to fall by such eyes. As a result, he became sad and confused. I spoke to Pathi Ji, who suggested that I should let him go home. I said okay, but Pathi Ji said that he is a strong-willed person and maybe he won't go back to his home and instead go somewhere else. Many times, before he received initiation, he would leave his home and family, and Pathi Ji would have to go and bring him back. So, I requested a dear one to do me the favor of accompanying him on a motorcycle to his village to make sure that he reached his home.

The mind always plays tricks with everyone. Kabir Sahib said, "O Kabir, this mind is a great trickster. If I say so, he gets angry. He doesn't tread on the path which makes him meet Almighty Lord." With whom has the mind not played tricks? Whom has he spared? He always tricks everyone. We talk about the *rishis* and *munis*, the sages and seers, but such things happen to us too.

When that dear one went back home, he didn't like being at home because one part of his mind was saying that he was wrong to leave me. With a long face he would just sit there, like a thief who is caught red-handed and feels as if he has done something very terrible. You know when a thief is caught red-handed, he does not have any way to escape. A few days later

God Will Call for Your Account

Pathi Ji came and told me about him. I told Pathi Ji, "Dear one, he is gone! No doubt he has kept renunciation in his mind, but outside such a thing is sitting that, whenever he will try to come out, he will be devoured by it. Kabir Sahib had said, 'One keeps his mind in renunciation, but in front keeps the woman. O Kabir, it is a bitter neem tree that he is nourishing, while he desires to eat sugar.' He wants to enjoy sugar but is watering the bitter neem tree. How will it work?"

Anyway, Pathi Ji did me a favor, and obeying me, he brought that dear one back to me. I saw his condition and it was exactly like a thief who has nowhere to escape and is caught red-handed. He told me, "It is not in my control. My wife loves me so much." I told him, "I have been watching you for the last thirty years and you both can't even stand each other. If this is called love, what would hatred be like?" When he came to me, I told him, "Dear one, now think about it and make up your mind. My beloved Master Kirpal thought for twelve to fourteen days about what he had to do with his life. Finally, he decided that God comes first, worldly affairs come next." I told him about my own history too. I told him, "Brother, it took me three years to make the decision to leave my home. I thought minutely about what problems I would have if I left home and what problems I would avoid if I left home. Once you set your foot on the battlefield, it is not good to withdraw." Kabir Sahib says, "If you become a householder maintain it as a religion, otherwise become a renunciate. If a renunciate gets caught in the bonds (of the world), he is a most unfortunate one." The mind tricks many great people.

Every day I am making you listen to the bani of Farid Sahib. Even if we start doing devotion, the mind does not leave us alone. He surrounds us with his weapons, the organs of senses.

Farid Sahib had a Pathan friend. Once the Negative Power came and sat within that friend to deceive Farid Sahib. This is because when we do meditation, Negative Power comes at us with full force. Farid Sahib was an advanced meditator and was connected with Naam within, but that Pathan was still under the influence of Negative Power. Negative Power thought that when delicious foods and women would be served to Farid Sahib, he would lose his concentration and would fall down. So, one day the Pathan

The Pain of Separation

presented Farid Sahib with delicious foods, women, etc. Seeing that, Farid Sahib said:

O Farid, these are poisonous sprouts coated with sugar.
Some die planting them, and some are ruined, harvesting and enjoying them.

When Vashishtha, the guru of Lord Rama, was imparting his teachings to Lord Rama, he said, "Whether one is a man or a woman, all have the same kind of organs of senses and the same things come out of them. From the eyes, dirt comes out; from the ears, dirt comes out; from the nose and the organs down below only filth and dirt come out, regardless of one being a man or a woman." He said, "It is a bag of dirt, foul smell comes out of it. It is filled only with dirt; don't understand it otherwise."

He said to beware of the organs of senses. Don't get stuck in them. That is why Mahatmas lovingly tell us that all bodies are made alike. Protect yourself from committing sins. Farid Sahib lovingly says, "I have told you as it is my responsibility. All bodies are made by the Negative Power and are covered with all the beautiful things which are like sugar. They are nothing but poison and he who tastes them will perish."

O Farid, four pahar[1] are lost wandering around, and four are lost in sleep.
God will call for your account and ask you why you came into this world.

Farid Sahib says, "Look here, O Dear One, someone leaves after getting married, someone leaves after getting engaged, somewhere a wife leaves, somewhere a husband goes away." Feeling sorry, he says, "You have spent four pahar (twelve hours) doing the works of the world, the other four pahar in sleep, but God Almighty will ask you for an account of every single breath he gave you. What will you reply to him at the time of judgment? You never remembered him nor did his devotion. When will you tell him that you remembered him? What are you doing? In which

---

[1] A watch, the unit of time in ancient India equal to three hours.

pursuits are you involved? Day and night, you think of bad things and do bad things."

O Farid, you have gone to the door of a palace. Have you seen the gong there?
This blameless object is being beaten; imagine what is in store for us sinners!

Once Farid Sahib went to a palace and at the door saw a gong. Usually they have gongs or bells at the entrance of palaces or temples. These are rung and, when this happens, they are getting a beating. In the old days, at the finish of every hour they would beat a bell. Farid says, "What mistake has it done, that it gets beaten all the time?" We are full of faults and the poor bell is innocent. When it gets a beating without doing anything bad, what will be our condition in the court of the Lord? He says, "The poor bell gets a beating every moment and gets even more at the finish of the hour. The same becomes the condition of the erring jivas in the court of the Lord. The Angels of Death give them a beating and punish them like this over there."

Each and every hour, it is beaten; it is punished every pahar.
This beautiful body is like a gong; it passes the night in pain.

Sheikh Farid has grown old, and his body has begun to tremble.
Even if he could live for hundreds of years, his body will eventually turn to
   dust.

Once an old man came to Sheikh Farid. He was trembling and he asked Farid Sahib for some remedy so that he could become young again. He was trembling even though it was not the cold season. Even without sitting on ice he was shivering. You know the body of an old person trembles and shivers even if it is not cold out. It is not in his control. Still the mind desires a long life and wants to regain its youth. You know once youth is lost, old age comes and one can never become young again. Farid Sahib tells him, "Dear one, your body is trembling, you have become old. Even if you get to live for one hundred years, still in the end you will have to go to your grave and get buried in dust, you have to turn to dust."

The Pain of Separation

Farid begs, O Lord, do not make me sit at another's door.
If this is the way you are going to keep me, then go ahead and take the life
out of my body.

Responding to that old man Farid Sahib again prays to his Master, "O Lord, O Master, do not give me a place to sit at another's door. If you are going to make me suffer sitting at another's door, take this soul out from my body." What is another's door? What is another's home? This world is another's. Guru Nanak Sahib has also called this world as another's. "We are stuck in the house which we have to leave. But we do not worry about that home where we have to go and live." Dear one, have you ever cared for the place where you will have to go and reside? Everyone has to go. This is why Mahatmas lovingly say, "O Lord, I do not like to stay in this others' world, because one day we have to leave everything here and go from here. If you want to keep me involved in births and deaths, it is better you take this soul out of this body."

With the axe on his shoulder, and a bucket on his head, the blacksmith is
ready to cut down the tree.
Farid says, I long for my Lord; you long only for the charcoal.

Yesterday also I had said that there was one blacksmith by the name of Jassa and he was a friend of Farid Sahib. He would go to the place where Farid Sahib used to meditate to get wood for his furnace. One morning, with an axe on his shoulder and a bucket of water on his head, he came to the place where Farid Sahib was meditating. At that time Farid Sahib had become tired sitting, so he had gotten up and stood by the tree in order to avoid sleep, and in this way, he continued his devotion to the Lord. By meditating his body had become stiff like wood. Jassa the blacksmith had weak eyesight. When he came to the tree, he didn't see Farid Sahib and, in order to check the wood, he hit the body of Farid Sahib with the butt of the axe, thinking it was the tree. Farid Sahib's samadhi was disturbed and he said to Jassa, "Look here, O Dear One, you have a water pot on your head and an axe on your shoulder and here I am praying to my Lord.

God Will Call for Your Account

I want to meet him. I am praying to him to grant me his darshan and you want to turn me into charcoal. What kind of friend are you?"

O Farid, some have lots of flour, while others do not even have salt.
When they go beyond this world, it shall be seen who will be punished.

Farid Sahib tells Jassa the blacksmith, "Look here, O Dear One, there are some who have lots of flour, while there are others who do not even have a little bit of salt; they don't know from where they will get their next meal." It means that there are some who have done so much meditation and have collected a lot of wealth (of meditation), but the others don't even have a little. God Almighty will ask for the accounts. Who will bear the beating? We know that when a thief is caught and is receiving a beating, who comes to his rescue? Guru Nanak Sahib says, "Over there a jiva is made to understand the accounts of his own deeds." He is told that these are your own deeds and now you have to suffer on account of them. So, Farid Sahib tells Jassa the blacksmith, "You do some repetition of Naam, meditate on Naam. You come to me every day. What will you tell God when you see him?"

Drums were beaten in their honor, there were canopies above their heads, and
  bugles announced their coming.
They have gone to sleep in the cemetery, buried like poor orphans.

Farid Sahib uttered this verse after witnessing a king's death. A king died and left all his palaces and mansions behind. I have seen this myself at the palaces of the kings in Punjab. In the evenings for two to three hours, they would play music to entertain the kings at the entrance of the palace. The musicians would play music; drums were beaten; bugles were blown. They used to have a special place made for the musicians, who would get very handsome salaries. So here he says, "The king has died and now no bugle is blown, no instrument is played. His house (palace) is abandoned and like an orphan he is put in the grave. He has left everything of this world here."

The Pain of Separation

O Farid, those who built houses, mansions and lofty buildings are also gone.
They made false deals, and were dropped into their graves.

Very lovingly Farid Sahib says, "First of all, neither those who built these mansions and palaces avoided death, nor the ones who live in them now will avoid death. Those who have made these places as their own properties, even they won't avoid death. It is only because of their ego and pride that they think otherwise. After living in them for a few days and indulging in vices for a few days, in the end they will have to die; it is a false business they have done." Farid Sahib only means to tell us that Masters come to connect us with Almighty Lord. They don't come to connect us with worldly properties because they know, as Master Kirpal used to say, that even this body in which we live is like a rented house; we can't even take this with us. So how can we take the worldly homes with us?

Up until now no one has become the owner of the world or worldly properties forever. After Jaimini Muni had written a famous book, in order to test him, his master Ved Vyas went to him in the disguise of a woman. When that woman took possession of his cottage and did not allow him to enter it, he said, "Why are you not opening the door of my cottage for me? It is my property. How can you not let me in?" Ved Vyas replied, "You say you are a great rishi and have written this great book. Don't you even know that no one can become the owner of this earth and of the maya (material possessions)?" This is why Masters tell us that these things do not have any owners. Our ancestors vomited them up and left, and here we are, licking them. We have forgotten the times when these worldly mansions did not accompany our ancestors. In what kind of illusion are we living?

O Farid, there are many seams on the patched coat, but there are no seams on the soul.
The sheikhs and their disciples have all departed, each in his own turn.

There was a fakir who was mending his coat, thinking that God will be met when one lives in such kind of poverty and humility. Farid Sahib tells him, "Dear one, you are putting so many seams on your coat. Have you ever mended this body, have you ensured that this body will stay here forever? No one stays in this world forever. Neither those who have supernatural powers, nor those who are wise. Everyone has to leave this world one day."

> *O Farid, while the two lamps (eyes) are (still) lit, the owner (the Angel of Death) has come anyway.*
> *He has captured the fortress of the body and plundered the home of the heart; he extinguishes the lamps and departs.*

The fakir who was patching his coat asked Farid Sahib, "Farid Sahib, is it true that the Angel of Death comes while the soul is still watching? Or does he come discreetly and then kill?" Farid Sahib told him, "No, dear one, both the sun and moon would be present. These two lamps, our eyes, would be lit and would be seeing, and the Angel of Death will come and take over this body, extinguish these two eyes and they won't be able see this world again. He does not fear anyone; that is why he comes openly."

> *O Farid, look at what has happened to the cotton and the sesame seed,*
> *The sugar cane and paper, the clay pots and the charcoal.*

The fakir further questioned Farid, "Does a soul really suffer in the court of the Lord?" The eyes of the Mahatmas are opened. They have knowledge of several births. They know what one became in which birth and they know how many wives or husbands we made and left. That is why Farid says "You see, dear one, even in this world you see with your own eyes that sugar cane is very strong but look at its condition. The farmers first cut it, which is very painful, and then peel its skin, which is torturous. Then it is crushed in a mill to obtain juice. The crushed stalks are burned in the fire, the juice gets boiled; how much pain does it suffer to become sweet sugar cane juice?" It is possible the souls in those sugar cane stalks were human beings in their previous births and now they are going through these sufferings on account of the bad karmas done in the human birth. Look at the condition of the cotton seeds. How much do they suffer to become a dress? First, they endure heat and thirst as a plant

The Pain of Separation

and then, after the cotton is produced, as cotton they suffer the beating of the looms and machines. As a cloth they get cut by the scissors of the tailors and then go through sewing machines in order to finally become a dress. It is possible that the souls in the cotton seeds were good souls in the past. But since they did not appreciate their human birth and did not do the devotion of God, their condition became like this. Also, he says to look at the condition of paper, clay and charcoal. Guru Nanak Sahib had said, "In order to become a pot, clay has to go through a lot of suffering. It is put on a wheel, cut with a string and baked in an oven." Is it easy? All things have life in them, and all living beings have knowledge. But we say, "No, it is just a talk." No, it is not like that.

When we go within, we come to know. When I took Baba Bishan Das, from whom I received initiation into the first Two Names, to see Baba Sawan Singh Ji, a Muslim fakir by the name of Fatti accompanied us. Fatti lived in the same village as Baba Bishan Das and he was a good fakir. He was not a so-called fakir; he was a meditator and used to go within. When we met with Baba Sawan Singh Ji, Fatti told him, "Master, one of your previous births was as the king of Faridkot." Master Sawan Singh Ji smiled and said, "I have also seen severe poverty in many of my previous births." You can see how much experience the Masters have and how they keep it hidden. Further Baba Sawan Singh Ji said, "If I go to the palace and claim ownership, will they even allow me to enter?"

The sugar cane and paper, the clay pots and the charcoal
This is the punishment for those who do evil deeds.

Now Farid says, "What is the condition of charcoal?" When it is made, it is painful. First the wood is burned, which is very painful. Then water is thrown on it, which also is very painful. It is like when we burn our hand and then cold water is thrown on top of the burn, how painful that is! After charcoal is made, again it is burned as fuel. This is why Farid Sahib says, "These are the punishments that those souls, who did bad karma in the human births and did not do bhajan and simran, suffer in these forms."

God Will Call for Your Account

O Farid, you wear your prayer shawl on your shoulders and the robes of a
Sufi; your words are sweet, but there is a dagger in your heart.
Outwardly, you look bright, but your heart is dark as night.

There was a fake sadhu. He used to talk in a very intellectual way. Farid Sahib told him, "You have put the meditation shawl on your shoulder, but within your heart is a dagger to kill others. On your lips you have sweet words like jaggery. You look bright from outside but within your heart is pitch darkness."

Once there were two persons who were expert in telling lies. They thought about how to deceive people and plunder the wealth of others. One said, "It is very simple; you justify my lie and I will justify yours." Together they went to a king and presented themselves as great mahatmas. They also said that in the past they used to be hunters. The king asked them to tell him about some extraordinary thing they had done. The first person said, "O Lord, I have shot the ear, foot and horn of a deer with one arrow." The king said, "This is a total lie. It is not possible." But the other person at once said, "No, my lord. You don't know him. He is a great archer. At the time he shot the arrow, the deer was scratching his ear with his foot. The horns had also come in line with the target as the deer's head was tilted." Now you see it was a total lie but they made it true. Then the king asked the second person, "Okay, now you tell me what you have done." He said, "Once I shot a pigeon, who was sitting on the branch of a tree, but it came down in my hands as a roasted pigeon." Now the king said, "No, no. This is a lie. It is not possible." But the first person said, "O Lord, it is not a lie. He is a great archer too. What happened was that before he shot the pigeon, the pigeon had eaten some coals and as the arrow hit the pigeon it sparked the coals and the fire was created, which roasted it before it fell on the ground." Again, it was a lie but because of their trick they made it sound true.

So, this is our condition. Paltu Sahib says, "He who has ten or twenty people with him, is called by the name *Mahant* (Master)." Those who collect a few followers, they always have such people with them, who turn lies into truth. They say, "Oh, this mahatma sees so much. When he closes his eyes, he can see up to the three worlds." Once Guru Nanak Dev Ji Maharaj went to Kurukshetra, a place of pilgrimage in India. He saw a person who would close his eyes, then open them and then close them again. He told Bhai Mardana and Bhai Bala that this person was a fake sadhu. He closes his eyes to impress people that he is a mahatma. Then he opens his eyes to see how much he has got in his cup and to make sure that no one has taken his money from the cup. People were praising him so much, saying that he can see up to the three worlds. Guru Nanak Dev Ji told Bhai Bala to take the sadhu's money cup and put it behind the sadhu. Guru Nanak Dev Ji himself sat in front of the sadhu with both of his hands folded. When the sadhu opened his eyes, he did not see his money cup and he got angry with Guru Nanak Dev Ji, saying that he had taken the sadhu's money cup. Guru Nanak Dev Ji smiled and said, "Neither do you have any knowledge nor do you do any yoga. Just to impress people you sometimes touch your ears.[2] You claim to see as far as three worlds, but you don't even know that your money cup is behind you." When the sadhu heard that, he became embarrassed.

Mahatmas lovingly say that people have sweet words on their tongue but daggers in their heart. They have followers who make their lies sound true. In their hearts there is pitch darkness, but they claim to be all light. They know nothing of this world but still claim to be the knower of all. This is not good as the sadhu should present himself exactly the way he is within.

Mr. Oberoi has written a book in English and in one of its chapters is written the story of Sunder Das. He was an initiate of Baba Sawan Singh Ji and he used to meditate with me. Once we were meditating in our fields and had some fire burning around us to keep us warm. He didn't have any blanket on his legs. A piece of burning wood fell on his leg and the leg got burnt, but he didn't realize it. When we got up from meditation, I saw his leg; it was completely burnt. I became very upset but he was very happy and told me that never in his life had he enjoyed meditation so much as he

---

[2] In Indian culture, touching the ears is a sign of repentance and sincerity.

God Will Call for Your Account

did on that day. I took him to Doctor Kapur Singh, who said that the leg would have to be cut off. We felt very sorry. Our beloved Master Kirpal used to visit me often. When he came and saw the leg, he told us, "There is no need to operate on the leg. Just wash it with neem water and apply limewater to it." After some time, his leg healed. Later Sunder Das asked many questions of Master Kirpal Singh Ji. He asked, "Would those who, becoming false masters, do the acting and posing, who deceive others and who enjoy delicacies, will they get any punishment?" Master Kirpal replied, "If I tell you anything, the dear ones sitting here won't be convinced. Close your eyes and see it for yourself and then tell the others." Master Kirpal Singh Ji made him have inner experiences many times, and he told us how there were so many false masters who were being punished within. He told how they were bleeding while being churned in the mill and how they were being eaten up by animals.

Mahatmas lovingly tell us that there is no sin greater than deceiving someone's soul: "The killer of a soul is a grave sinner."

So like Farid Sahib has said, we should also become pure, sincere and truthful in our within. We should do the meditation of Shabd Naam, so that looking at our sincerity God Almighty may open his door for us. Supreme Father Kirpal used to say, "Truth is above all, but higher still is True Living."

Chapter 5

The Days Are Passing

On the first day of the program I said that every day I will be doing satsang on the bani of Sufi Saint Farid. So today, like every day, his bani is presented to you. Sufi means having a pure heart, where only Naam exists. It means that one has a heart where there is no hatred for anyone because one understands that God resides within everyone.

Farid Sahib had many experiences in his life and he remained in meditation a lot. In the beginning he didn't have the path of Shabd Naam and he wandered in the forests a great deal. One day he was returning from the forest and was very hungry. He will mention this again later on in his bani saying, "O Farid, hunger is worse than death. One sleeps after eating but when he wakes up, it is standing there again." We eat in the morning but in the evening, we want to eat again. We eat in the evening, but again the next morning we are hungry. On the way where Farid was walking some man had thrown away the skins of a melon after eating the fruit. Farid Sahib picked up those melon skins and ate them because he was very hungry. Suddenly the man who had thrown away the melon skins came back to that place and said, "I dropped my knife here, give it back to me." Farid Sahib told him, "Brother, I did eat the skins you left but I have not seen or taken the knife. If I had seen it, I would have called you and given it to you." However, that person did not believe Farid Sahib and kept on accusing him of taking the knife. You know that when someone wants to show off his

The Pain of Separation

power and ego, no matter what you say or do to prove yourself right, he will not listen to you nor believe you. So, out of his egoism that man started giving a beating to Farid Sahib. Farid Sahib endured the beating and started laughing. The man asked Farid Sahib, "I am beating you, why are you laughing?" Farid Sahib said, "One gets as many diseases as the enjoyments he has had. If one gets a beating for eating the skins, what happens to those who eat the fruit?" He said, "I am laughing because I ate only the skins and got a beating. What would have happened if I had eaten the fruit?"

In today's bani Farid Sahib says that one should do so much meditation, so many *tapas* (austerities), that blood should not remain present within his body. If his body were to be cut, there should be no blood; only water should come out. Some disciples put this question to Guru Amar Dev, "Master, it is written in Farid's bani that one should do so much tapas and meditation that no blood should remain in the body, and if one were to cut the body only water should come out and not blood. Is this correct? Or does it need some changes?" Guru Amar Dev Ji did not criticize Farid Sahib. He lovingly explained to his disciples, "You see, the body cannot exist without blood, but those who do the devotion of Lord, from within them the blood of greed goes away because they always fear Lord Almighty. They are always scared of death and of the time when they will be asked to settle the accounts of their karmas. That is why the blood of greed vanishes from their being, just like gold becomes pure after going through the heat of fire. In the same way, by doing the devotion of Lord, their body becomes pure."

Guru Amar Dev then told the disciples a very good story. There was a rishi whose name was Kumutt. He was doing his practices in the forest. Once, when he got up from his meditation a thorn pricked his foot. He removed the thorn but not even one drop of blood came out, as all his life he had lived in the forest doing his austerities and meditations. When he saw that no blood came out from his wound, he became very proud of himself. He became happy and started dancing in happiness. Seeing him happy and dancing, the other creatures in the forest also started dancing with him. When the gods saw this, they requested Lord Shiva to take care of it. They said, "O Lord, you have done so many tapas and you are the best *tapasvi* (one who does the tapas or austerities), but this rishi has become proud that he is the best." In order to quiet them down Lord Shiva came to that rishi and asked him why he was so happy and full of pride. He replied, "I am a great tapasvi. I have no blood in my body. There is no one greater than me." Lord Shiva told him, "Dear one, it is not good to be proud of oneself as those who are full of ego get killed." It is said that in order to break his ego, Lord Shiva cut a part of his (own) body to show him that even in his body there was no blood. Lord Shiva told him, "The purpose of doing tapas and meditation practices is to develop humility and not egoism."

O Farid, not even a drop of blood would come out, if someone cut my body.
Those bodies which are imbued with the Lord, they contain no blood.

Shloka of Guru Amar Das:

This body is all blood; without blood, this body could not exist.
Those who are imbued with their Lord do not have the blood of greed in their bodies.
When the fear of God fills the body, it becomes thin; the blood of greed departs from within.
Just as metal is purified by fire, the fear of God removes the filthy residues of evil-mindedness.
O Nanak, those humble beings are beautiful, who are imbued with the Lord's love.

Guru Amar Das Ji Maharaj lovingly explained to them, saying, "Dear ones, a body cannot exist without blood, but those who get connected with Shabd within, those who are connected with Lord Almighty, from their within the blood of greed disappears. They become pure like gold becomes pure from the heat of the fire. They look good and beautiful in the court of the Lord and they are glorified there."

O Farid, seek that sacred pool in which the genuine article is found.
What would happen if you search in the pond? Your hand will only sink into the mud.

The Pain of Separation

Farid Sahib says to go into such people's company where one's life may become perfect, one's forgetful mind may divert its attention towards Lord Almighty, and one may do the devotion of Lord Almighty. Masters tell us that the company we keep has a profound effect on us. If we are in bad people's company, we inculcate bad qualities. If we are in good people's company, we develop good qualities. Mahatmas lovingly explain to us that it is like a swan who sits in a pond and puts his beak into the dirty water of that pond. He gets nothing but dirt. Farid Sahib is giving its example and says, "O Brother, go to that sacred pool where your food is, where the pearls are. What are you going to get in this dirty pond?" In the same way the Masters tell us that we should also go in good company, derive the benefit from there and make our lives successful.

> *O Farid, when she is young, she does not enjoy her Husband. When she grows up, she dies.*
> *Lying in the grave, the soul-bride cries, "I did not meet you, my Lord!"*

Now he lovingly says that as long as youth is present, it is time to do the devotion of the Lord. The soul has life in this body and she has to make her life successful by doing devotion. When that soul goes in the grave, she wishes and prays to meet God and for God to forgive her.

> *O Farid, your hair has turned gray, your beard has turned gray, and your moustache has turned gray.*
> *O my thoughtless and insane mind, why are you indulging in pleasures?*

Farid Sahib lovingly says, "You see, dear one, your hair has turned gray, your beard has turned gray, and also your moustache has turned gray. But your mind is still not coming towards Lord Almighty. It only goes towards the pleasures and towards the world."

> *O Farid, how long can you run on the rooftop? You are asleep to your Husband Lord; give it up!*
> *The days which were allotted to you are numbered, and they are passing, passing away.*

The Days Are Passing

Now Farid Sahib lovingly says if a person gets on a rooftop, how far can he run there? Twenty or fifty feet, that is it. There is no space for him to go further. The same is the condition of our existence. God Almighty has given you a specific number of days, a limited number of breaths. Don't waste them following your forgetful mind. The life span of this body is a few years. Some lives are finished in childhood and some are finished in adolescence. Later old age comes and the cough, pains in the joints and various other diseases will surround you. Where is there to go further after this? This life is short.

> *O Farid, houses, mansions and balconies, do not attach your consciousness to these.*
> *Immeasurable amount of dust will be put on you when you die, and no one will be your friend.*

Now he lovingly says that you are in love with your houses and mansions. You wish that your houses and mansions would be the best, the highest, the strongest and with the best engravings. But what will our attachment to these things do? It is a pity that in the end, whether one is a king or a subject, and even if he is the owner of a community, he will only receive an immeasurable amount of dust. We know that when we are buried in the grave, we are covered under dust which cannot be measured. If we are cremated, we are reduced to just a heap of dust, which is so little that it also cannot be measured.

> *O Farid, do not focus on mansions and wealth; center your consciousness on death, your powerful enemy.*
> *Think of that place where you have to go.*

Now Farid Sahib gives us a warning. He says, do not get attached to the mansions, homes, properties, possessions and material things of this world. Care for and think about the place where you have to go and live after death. Over there neither your mother nor brothers, nor sisters, nor friends will be with you. Only the deeds which you do here will be your companion. Further he will explain to us in detail about the deeds which we do here. "The deeds we do in this world come to our rescue in the court of the Lord." Dear brothers, only those deeds will be useful. That is why

The Pain of Separation

lovingly he says, "You will have no companion over there. Only your deeds and actions will be your companion."

> *O Farid, forget those deeds which do not bring merit.*
> *Otherwise, you will be put to shame in the court of the Lord.*

Now he lovingly says to leave those affairs which do not have merit in them, so that you will not feel embarrassed in the court of the Lord. Mahatmas tell us a story: once there was a prostitute who told her servant to go and find out whether a person in the neighborhood who had just died had gone to the heavens or to the hells. A Mahatma was passing by her house and he heard this conversation. He wondered how not only a prostitute but even her servant could have such knowledge about where a dead person had gone. He thought, "Let me find out what is going on in here." So, he sat there and after some time the servant came back and said, "He has gone to the heavens." Upon hearing this the Mahatma asked her, "Dear daughter, please tell me: how do you know whether the dead person has gone to the heavens or hells?" She replied, "I have heard from some Mahatma that if a person is praised after his death, he surely has gone to the heavens. If a person is cursed after his death and people say, 'It is good that he has died as he used to torture and trouble others,' certainly such a person has gone to the hells." So that is why Farid Sahib says, "Don't do such things which do not have any merit in them and which will not help you. Do such deeds which will not make you feel embarrassed after going to the court of the Lord."

> *O Farid, serve the Master; dispel the doubts of your heart.*
> *The dervishes[1] have the patient endurance of trees.*

Farid Sahib says, "Do the devotion of the Lord. First of all, you should have faith that what you are doing is right and that the Lord will accept it. Do not waver. Sometimes you say you will meet with the Lord, other times you say you won't. Give up this unfaithfulness. Lord Almighty definitely meets with those who have firm faith and determination. God Almighty gives them a

---

[1] Member of Sufi religious order, who has taken vows of poverty and austerity.

place in his home." Further he says, "The dervishes have the patient endurance of trees." It is very difficult to become a devotee of God, a dervish of God. Kabir Sahib said, "O Kabir, (doing) fakiri (devotion of God) is far away, just like dates on the date tree. If one climbs it, he gets the fruit of immortality, otherwise falling down he is broken into pieces." What are the Beloveds of God like? What are dervishes like? They are just like a heap of dirt. A heap of dirt does not feel bad if someone throws dirt on it, nor does it feel bad if someone throws good things on it. It doesn't feel bad and it doesn't curse them. It quietly endures all kinds of treatment. Farid Sahib gives the example of trees, which are the same way. A tree doesn't mind if anyone cuts it, throws stones at it or waters it. It only gives fruit. It doesn't curse anyone. In the same way, Hazrat Bahu says, "Wear the garment of a Fakir if you want to die while living. Like a heap of dirt, endure the dirt and other things which they throw on you. Even if someone calls you names, respect them." It is for each person to decide how he wants to treat a Saint. It is his own understanding, but Saints lovingly welcome both those who come with devotion and those who come with ill feelings towards them. Everyone has his own angle of vision and his own feelings. Saints only see God Almighty in everyone. They don't see any difference between a man and a woman. They don't have any hatred for anyone. They love all.

O Farid, my clothes are black, and my outfit is black.
I wander around full of sins, and yet people call me a dervish.

Saints, the Beloveds of God, do not come into this world to justify themselves. They come to teach us love and humility. They do not tell us that they are the true ones or the pure ones. Instead they say, "Brothers, we are the worst of sinners." Kabir Sahib said, "I went to look for a sinner, but couldn't find one. When I looked within my heart, I found that no one was worse than me." This doesn't mean that Kabir Sahib was a bad person. No, Saints teach us humility and meekness. They tell us, "Brothers, God Almighty doesn't love egoism. He loves humility." Our Satguru Maharaj Kirpal used to say, "If you want to meet with God, bring humility with you because he is the owner of everything except humility. In front of whom can he be humble?"

In those days, sadhus or fakirs, the devotees of God, used to wear

The Pain of Separation

black-colored clothes. Later on, it changed to white and then to saffron and many other colors. That is why here he says, "O Farid, my clothes are black, and my outfit is black. I wander around full of sins, and yet people call me a dervish, a holy man. People call me a fakir but I feel embarrassed as I have many shortcomings in me." Guru Nanak Sahib also says, "Neither have I earned the *japa* (repetition), tapa, (maintained) continence and (followed) religion, nor have I known service to the Sadhus, O Lord. Nanak says, I am of lowest karmas. Please liberate me who has taken refuge in you." If there is anyone who can make the life of a disciple, it is his Master. As long as the Master is in the body, he never has ego that he is learned or the owner of any skill. He never says that he has meditated or possesses any power. He always keeps love and humility in his heart.

> *The crop which is burnt will not bloom, even if it is soaked in water.*
> *O Farid, she who is forsaken by her Husband Lord grieves and laments.*

Now, giving a very good example, he lovingly says, "Just like when a crop dries and is burnt, even if you make it stand in water it will not become green again. New green leaves will not grow in that crop because it is burnt." In the same way those souls who do not understand after coming in the satsang, in the end they will grieve. They will grieve and lament and feel sorry, saying, "Oh! Why didn't I listen to the Masters and do the meditation of Shabd Naam? Why didn't I divert my mind from the wrong path and involve it in the right path? Why did I waste my life?"

> *When she is a virgin, she is full of desire; but when she is married, then her troubles begin.*
> *O Farid, she has this one regret, that she cannot be a virgin again.*

Whether one is a man or a woman, as long as we are unmarried, we have the desire to get married. However, when we get married and have children, many problems come up, such as taking care of the children, paying for their studies and other expenses, getting them married, etc. Sometimes in those painful situations one thinks, "Had I known all this would happen, I would not have gotten married." But what can be done? That time has gone out of one's hands. Saints and Mahatmas do not advise us to be weak. They say that now, when you have entered family life, whatever responsibilities God Almighty has given to you, responsibilities that you had gladly asked for, happily attend to them and don't get bewildered. In the same way, when a disciple gets Naam initiation, he has the thought and desire to somehow meditate so much that, taking his attention above the level of mind and the organs of the senses, he connects it with Shabd Naam. He is anxious and says, "When will I open the inner veil and have the darshan of the Light and of my Master?" When he lovingly collects his scattered attention, concentrates and reaches the *tisra til* (third eye), God Almighty is not unjust. He opens the inner veil. We know that to him whose inner veil is opened, he gives many jobs to do, like connecting to the Lord those souls who are yet not connected and giving the message of God to them. Giving the message of God Almighty is the most difficult job. Kabir Sahib says, "God Almighty has sent me to deliver a message to the souls to come home, which Kabir gives with much difficulty." He says that God Almighty gave him the job of calling people to come back home, but he had to give out that message in this world with much difficulty. You already know Kabir Sahib's history and how many pains and difficulties people gave him. They tortured him. So, one whose inner veil has opened repents. He says, "The Master surely liberates those whom he initiates. Why did I meditate so much? Had I known that giving out his message was so difficult, I would have not done so much meditation." But what can be done then? Guru Nanak Sahib says, "Once the Master takes someone in his refuge, he never leaves him."

A swan landed in a small pond of salt water.
He dipped his beak in it, but did not drink; he flew away, still thirsty.

Now he gives the example of a swan who came to a dirty pond and tried to find his food, pearls. He found only dirt and he thought to himself, "Let me not put my beak any further into this water. Let me fly away." Similarly, the Beloveds of God Almighty come into this world and do not get involved in the dirt of this world. Once a swan went to a field of millet, and the owner of that field gave him a hard time. The farmer did not know

The Pain of Separation

that swans don't care for millet; it is not their food. In the same way, when the Beloveds of God come in this world to teach us love and humility, we chase them away and bother them thinking that they have come to take something from us. We don't realize that Masters do not come to grab our properties and possessions. They come for a few days and live like a traveler. They know that God will call them back one day and they will have to leave. They say, "No one knows whether the breath we have taken in will come out or not." We worldly people do not know how long others are going to live in this world nor how long we are going to live in this world.

In Punjab there is a village by the name Sanguwala. It is a deserted village and not many people live there. When I went there, I saw only a few houses and the ruins of a fort. What I heard from the people there was that about two hundred years ago a sadhu used to live in that village. In those days there used to be many groups of thieves in that area and so the villagers wanted to build a fort to protect themselves from the thieves. People living in different homes were unsafe so they wanted to make a fort for the entire village. They asked the sadhu to move the place where he used to stay and meditate. In reply the sadhu asked them to move the wall of the fort a little bit so that he would not be disturbed, but they insisted on building the wall right where they wanted. That poor sadhu did not want to go through the trouble of rebuilding his place so he requested them many times to move the fort slightly back. They got angry and asked him, "Are you the owner of this land?" He replied, "No, I am not, but it will help me a lot if I stay where I am. It won't make much difference to you, if you would move the fort a little bit." The villagers did not listen to the sadhu and got angry. In order to punish him for not obeying them, they tied him to a pair of bullocks and made those bullocks drag him around the village. As a result, he died. That sadhu did not curse them. He did tell them, however, "Neither will your homes increase in number nor will mine stay here forever." It is the law of nature that one has to pay for all the bad deeds one does. It is said that the villagers there originally had only had eight homes. A ninth one never got built. I have seen this myself. The meaning of saying this is that the Beloveds of God come into this world like swans, who do not want worldly things. Just like the farmers

The Days Are Passing

chased the swan out of the field of millet, without knowing that he had not come for that, in the same way we bother the Masters when they come.

> *The swan flew away and landed in the fields of millet. The people go to chase him away.*
> *The thoughtless people do not know that swans do not eat millet.*
>
> *The birds which inhabit the pools will fly away and leave.*
> *O Farid, the overflowing pool shall also perish, and only the lotus flowers shall remain.*

Now he says that the owners of many properties and of forts with deep foundations developed those properties but left empty-handed. We will also leave empty-handed. Nam Dev Ji writes in his bani, "One hundred brothers of Duryodhana, the Kauravas, used to boast, 'Mine, mine.' They had a vast canopy over their heads, but their bodies were not eaten, even by the vultures. Ravana had his kingdom, Lanka, made of gold. Who could be bigger than him? He had his state protected by an army of elephants, but he lost it in one moment."

> *O Farid, a stone will be your pillow, and the earth will be your bed. The worms shall eat into your flesh.*
> *Countless ages will pass, and you will still be lying on one side.*

Now he lovingly says, "You see, dear one, in the place of fluffy silk pillows you will get a brick or stone as your pillow. The worms will eat your flesh. No one is going to wake you up from that sleep. No one knows how much time will go by like that." Kabir Sahib says, "When we are cremated, we are reduced to ashes, and if we are buried an army of ants eat us up." Farid Sahib also says the same thing: that you will get a stone for a pillow, the worms will eat you up, and no one will wake you up. They will not even move you and who knows how long you will be lying on one side.

> *O Farid, your beautiful body shall break apart, and the subtle rosary of the breath shall be snapped.*
> *In which house will the Messenger of Death be a guest today?*

The Pain of Separation

Farid Ji says that this body is very good; it is very beautiful, and everyone loves it. The rosary of breaths is moving within this body but one day it is going to break. Who knows in whose home the Angel of Death will come as a guest in order to take that person away? No one has any control over the Angel of Death. He says that one day the rosary of breaths will be snapped. We know that we shall still have eyes in this beautiful body, but our vision shall be lost, and we won't be able to blink those eyes. We shall have a tongue in our mouth, but it won't speak like it is speaking now. In the same way, we will still have legs on our body, but they won't move. Unless God Almighty moves the rosary of breaths in our body, this beautiful body of ours does not function. Graciously God Almighty has given us this beautiful priceless body. You know that when we lose one of our eyes, no matter what we are willing to pay, no one will give his eye to us. We cannot get the same kind of eye at any cost. In the same way, when we lose a leg or a hand, even though nowadays prosthetics are available, they are nothing like what God Almighty gave us. I have met with many dear ones who have had eye surgery done. I would ask them how their vision was and they told me that it was good. After I had eye surgery, the surgeon asked me how my vision was. I told him, "I can see well but it is not as clear as it was before." He said, "Master, we cannot replace natural eyes. The eyes which God Almighty gave us cannot be replaced by any technique." So that is why Mahatmas lovingly tell us, "Dear ones, graciously God Almighty has given you this beautiful form. Due to the presence of the rosary of breaths he granted us, everyone—mother, father, brother, sister, friends—respects and loves us. But when that rosary's movement stops, no one values us. They don't want to keep us (our body) even for a moment." Kabir Sahib says, "When the *pranas* (breaths) are separated from the body, they call him a ghost. They don't keep him even for a moment and the family members take him out (for cremation or burial)."

> *O Farid, your beautiful body shall break apart, and the subtle rosary of the breath shall be snapped.*
> *Those friends who were a burden on the earth, how can they come today?*

Now he says, "Once the rosary of breaths is snapped within, which people become a burden on this earth?" Those who go on saying "I, I" all day,

The Days Are Passing

who do not do the devotion of Lord, and who neither give good advice to others nor accept it for themselves, become a burden on this earth. Kabir Sahib said, "Be scared of those who are devoid of doing the Lord's devotion." Only those people are a burden on the earth. He says that good as well as bad people have to go away from this world, but the difference between them is known once we reach the court of the Lord. Some are glorified and others are insulted and suffer.

Farid says, O faithless dog, this is not a good way of life.
You never come to the mosque for your five daily prayers.

Now he lovingly says, "Have you ever come inside the mosque?" The only purpose of going to these religious places we have made, call them mosque, temple or *gurdwara*,[2] is to live up to what we hear over there and to maintain their sanctity. Mahatmas made these places so that after doing our worldly chores we may go there and do some devotion of the Lord, do the meditation. Lovingly he says that they were not made only for rites and rituals. They were made for our improvement and our progress. So, Farid Sahib asks that dear one, "Did you even enter your mosque? Did you care for cleaning your mosque?" In the Muslim community it is necessary to go to the mosque five times a day and do the five *namaz* (prayers). Guru Nanak Sahib says, "Perform the five namaz, meditate on the five Names and wear the five attributes." Clean your intentions, quiet your heart, live on honest earnings, make your heart as soft as wax and have mercy for all beings: these are attributes one should have in the rosary he moves. He said, "You are a man and it doesn't look good that you don't do the devotion of God Almighty who has created you. You should do his devotion."

Rise up, O Farid, and cleanse yourself; chant your morning namaz.
Chop off and remove that head which does not bow to the Lord.

Now Farid Sahib tells us, "Dear ones, get up in the morning. If you

---

[2] Sikh place of worship.

The Pain of Separation

cannot take a complete bath, do the *panch-snana* (washing five organs of the body, the hands, feet, eyes, ears and nose)." We call it *panch-snana* and the Muslims call it *oojuu*. Farid Sahib says, "Rise up in the ambrosial hour, do the devotion of Lord and join him." He then asks, "What is the use of a head which doesn't bow down to the Lord at that time? It should be chopped off." You see that even birds and animals rise up in the morning and remember God in their own language. Farid Sahib says, "I sacrifice myself on those birds, who live in the forests and wilderness, who do not have any protection from storms and winds and who even get killed in them, but still they remember the Lord in their own way."

> *That head which does not bow to the Lord, what is to be done with that head?*
> *Put it in the fireplace, instead of firewood.*

Farid Sahib is not taunting anyone; he is saying this for himself. He says that a head which doesn't bow down to the Lord should be cut and burnt in the fireplace. Muslims get upset when burning a body is even mentioned, but Farid Sahib doesn't even worry about his own community's likes and dislikes. He only cares for his own improvement.

> *O Farid, where are your mother and father who gave birth to you?*
> *They have left you, but even so, you are not convinced that you shall also have*
> *to go.*

Farid Sahib says, "Think about this patiently: you are proud of your family thinking that it is greater than everyone else's and that others are lower than you. Just think about it. Where are your parents who were born in the same family? When they left, they did not even tell you where they were going; they just left." Often, I say that when a death occurs in a family, neither the father consults with his son, nor the son consults with his mother. When the time comes, we all go our own way. Farid Sahib says that when a death occurs, we ourselves carry the dead body on our shoulders to the cremation ground, but then we forget that one day the same thing will happen to us too. We think that death is only for others and maybe this time will not come for us. That is why here Farid Sahib says, "Where are your parents who gave you birth? They have left you and still your heart is not touched so that you think that you should do the devotion of the Lord and become his Beloved."

O Farid, flatten out your mind; smooth out the hills and valleys.
Hereafter, the fires of hell shall not even approach you.

Someone came to Farid Sahib and asked him to tell him the way through which one can meet God and do his devotion. He said, "First of all, clean and level off the ground of your mind; level off whatever forts lust, anger, greed, attachment and egoism have built within you. If those faults are not leaving you alone, just turn your back towards them. Then you will not have to face the fire of the hells."

Shloka of Guru Arjan Dev:

O Farid, the Creator is in the creation, and the creation abides in God.
Whom can we call bad? There is none without Him.

Now this is the bani of Guru Arjan Dev Ji Maharaj. He says, "O Farid, the creation lives in the Creator and the Creator resides in the creation. Whom can we call bad, whom can we hate when nothing is sustained without the presence of God Almighty within it?" Just imagine if we hate someone, some religion or some community, we are hating God Almighty, because God Almighty resides within all. We should listen to the bani of the Mahatmas lovingly and understand it patiently. Why should we hate anyone? We don't know when the Negative Power will call us and when we will have to leave this world. Since the creation lives in the Creator and he resides within all, we should love all the creation, understanding it as the Creator himself.

Chapter 6

I Hope to See My Lord

After coming to this world, Saints and Mahatmas, the Beloveds of God, always give us the message that this is a fair from which everyone departs; no one stays here forever. We do not know how many wives, how many husbands and how many children we had and left in our previous births. We do not know how many homes we made and abandoned. We don't even know where we travelled to in our previous births. We do not remember any of those things. Even if one were to remember and go to enter the house he used to own in his previous birth, would the present owners allow him to enter it? No, they would say, "We don't know you. You are a thief or a thug."

Baba Bishan Das, from whom I received the knowledge of Two Words, was not satisfied with what he had spiritually. He used to say that the destination is beyond those two planes. At the time when I came to know about Baba Sawan Singh Ji, he was visiting the city of Peshawar and I was in the army, stationed at the cantonment of Nowshera. Later I took Baba Bishan Das to see Baba Sawan Singh Ji. There was a Muslim fakir by the name of Fatti, who used to live near by Baba Bishan Das, and he also accompanied us. When we got to the feet of Baba Sawan Singh Ji, many conversations took place. Baba Bishan Das told Master Sawan about me, that I had done so many rites and rituals, that I had performed austerities such as the practice of jaldhara, and that he had initiated me into Two Words. Baba Sawan

The Pain of Separation

Singh Ji heard all that and said that all jivas are involved in rites, rituals and austerities over many past births, but liberation is in Naam. He said that we cannot get Naam without the perfect Masters, because Naam is not just words. Master Sawan always used to say, "If Naam was just words, even a five-year-old girl, who spins the wheel to make cotton, could give it. No, Naam is attention and the Master installs Naam within us. No one else has the power or authority to do that. We know that only a wrestler can teach wrestling. Only he who goes within can take us there."

While we were there, Fatti told Master Sawan Singh Ji, "Master, one of your previous births was in the royal family of Faridkot (a state in undivided India)." Master Sawan said, "Yes, but I have also seen a tremendous amount of poverty in many births. If I go and lay claim on those palaces that I made and where I used to live, will they let me enter?"

Two kinds of people come into this world. One kind are those who tell us not to think of doing bad things to others, as God resides within everyone. If God Almighty has to reward anyone for good deeds, he himself will do it and if he has to punish anyone for bad deeds, it will be only him that does it. Why should one be worried about anyone else? The other kind of people are those who create divisions among people and then go. They make several gods according to their understanding. Nowadays, as you know, this is what is happening in society. In contrast, when Saints and Mahatmas come, they tell us, "We all have one God. The way and the means to realize him is one. We all are his children and he cannot be realized by doing outer rites and rituals. We meet him only after going within."

Go through the life histories of the Masters; read the life of Guru Nanak. He had parents, a wife and two children, but when the thought of meeting God Almighty came within him, he became practically successful in doing that. Later he gave the secret of Shabd Naam to people, free of charge. When it came to doing the devotion of God Almighty, he was not concerned about his wife or parents. He gave out this message openly to the entire world, "Dear ones, he who shows you your real home within your home (human body), know him as the all-knowing Satguru. The within where the five melodies are playing is the sign of the manifestation

I Hope to See My Lord

of Shabd." He said, "Who is a Saint? Who is a Guru or *Pir*[1]?" The perfect Masters, while they are in the body, never say that they are our Master or Guru or Pir. These labels do not mean anything. You may call them with any name you wish; call them a friend, call them a brother or call them by the name their parents gave to them. These outer things don't make any difference, but they do tell us, "Go within and see the truth with your own eyes."

Masters don't say that they have done it and we can't. Our Satguru Kirpal Singh Ji Maharaj used to say, "What a man has done, a man can do." From reading about the Masters, we come to know how much yearning they had for God realization. I often have said that if they were born in a rich family, they did not care for affluence. Rejecting wealth, they did the meditation of Shabd Naam. They did not consider the world higher than God. They considered God Almighty higher than the world. They did not worry about public shame. If they were born in poverty, even then they did not become a burden on others. They earned their living by honest means and lived on it. Ravidas Ji mended shoes all his life and served the sangat freely. Kabir Sahib wove on the loom even though the king of Balkh Bukhara was his disciple.

The coming of the king of Balkh Bukhara to Kabir Sahib happened like this: once he was sleeping in his palace and he heard some footsteps on the roof. He looked into it and found someone walking on the roof. He asked who he was and the person, who in fact was Kabir Sahib disguised as a shepherd, said, "I am a shepherd and I am looking for my lost camel." The king said, "This is a palace and not even a bird can fly over it. How can you expect to find a camel here?" Kabir Sahib replied, "In the same way you, sleeping on the bed made of flowers, expect to find God Almighty. You have yearning for him but is it possible to find him while enjoying the pleasures?" Hearing this the king became bewildered, as he was a good soul. The next morning, he woke up upset and went to court. There at court, Kabir Sahib came in a form of a very impressive man, who

---

[1] A Sufi teacher or spiritual Master.

The Pain of Separation

could not be stopped by the guards. He came all the way up to the king and said, "I want to spend a night in this traveler's inn." The king said, "Are you insane? This is a palace and not a traveler's inn." Kabir Sahib asked him who had made it, and the king replied that it was his father who had made it. Kabir Sahib then asked him, "Who stayed here before you and your father?" The king answered that his forefathers and many others lived there. Kabir Sahib said, "If they didn't stay here forever, if they all left, how can you expect to stay here forever? What is it then? Is it not a traveler's inn?" Then Kabir disappeared.

Mahatmas tell us that we have come empty-handed and will leave empty-handed too. Who are we relying upon? Who is going to help us in the beyond? This is the reason why the Masters have so much yearning to realize God Almighty in their within.

After Kabir Sahib disappeared, the king wanted to find a Mahatma who could help him find God. He asked his people if they knew of a Saint. He was told that in the city of Kashi there is one Saint who was a weaver by profession and his name is Kabir Sahib. At first public shame kept him from going to Kabir Sahib, but after some time he overcame it. He went to Kabir Sahib and asked him to give him something. Kabir Sahib asked him who he was and where he had come from. He replied, "I am the king of Balkh Bukhara." Kabir Sahib told him, "I am a poor weaver and you are the king of Balkh Bukhara. How will it work to have you stay with me?" Because he was a good soul and was desirous of knowing God Almighty, he said, "I will eat whatever dry or unbuttered food you will give me. I have not come here as a king but have come as a beggar. I will do the work you ask me to do, understanding it as worship." He served Kabir Sahib for six years like that and then one day Mata Loi, who used to help Kabir Sahib in serving the sangat, said, "He is a king but still he works for you. He eats whatever you give him; he has never complained. Please give him something." Kabir Sahib replied, "The vessel is not yet ready." How can we people know if the vessel is ready or not? We only look outside and, looking at the outside, decide when it is ready. However, time proves what one is like within. So, when Kabir Sahib said the vessel was not yet ready, Mata Loi said, "How can I know that is true?" Kabir Sahib asked her to take some vegetable peels, stand on the balcony, and throw the peels on the king when he was called in. When Kabir Sahib called the king, she threw the peels on him. He got very angry and said, "If we were in Balkh Bukhara, I would have punished you, you who threw these peels!" He said many other things in anger. Mata Loi said, "I understood him as a great humble lover of the Master, but look at him. What has he stored within himself?"

Another six years passed with the king living with Kabir Sahib. Mata Loi had already witnessed what he was like earlier, so what could she say about him? Kabir Sahib was the knower of inner secrets and one day he said, "Now the vessel is ready." She said, "How can I know that? He looks the same to me." Kabir Sahib said, "This time take dirty garbage and throw it on him." The king had gone through many experiences in those twelve years and now he knew that his body was full of garbage and filth. So, when she threw garbage on him, he looked up and said, "Bless you, the thrower of garbage. I am worse than this garbage; my mind is filled with filth." When Kabir Sahib saw that he was cleansed of ego, he gave him Naam initiation. Now you know that when one has yearning and one's within is clean, how much time does it take to realize God? It takes time only when one takes initiation but has no yearning for God and still has the same lust, anger, greed, etc., in one's within. If we use these things even more than before, how can Naam get manifested within us? How can Shabd manifest within us? If our within is filled with the whole world, where can he reside? This is why lovingly it is said that within the Beloveds of God, the Masters, there is a unique kind of yearning.

The bani of Farid Sahib is presented to you. Farid Sahib was a Sufi Saint, born in the Muslim religion, and his bani is included in the Guru Granth Sahib. Guru Arjan Dev Ji Maharaj has included the banis of only those Masters who had attained the highest position, had reached the eternal home and whose path was that of the Five Shabds. Farid had so much yearning in his within since his childhood. When he did so many rites and rituals and still did not get to meet the Lord, he had the pain of separation; one can understand the pain of separation only if one experiences it. He who does not know what the pain of separation is, how can he understand

The Pain of Separation

it? Here we weep for our children and wealth. The wife weeps for her husband and the husband weeps for his wife, but there are also such people who stay up all night in the separation of God Almighty and weep for him. Kabir Sahib says, "The whole world is happy, they eat and sleep. Servant Kabir is unhappy as he weeps and stays awake." He says, "I have the pain of separation from God and that is why I stay up and weep for him." In the same way Farid Sahib says, "O Farid, on the day I was born, if my mother had cut my throat instead of my umbilical cord, I would not have fallen into so many troubles and suffered so much." Just imagine if we all had the same thoughts like Farid Sahib; how would we still be sitting here? We would have met God Almighty right away. Master Kirpal used to say, "The coming of a dear soul to the Master is like bringing dry gunpowder near the fire." We, the others, are wet gunpowder and when we get the warmth of the satsangs, we dry up in respect to the desires of the world and we wake up in respect to God Almighty. So, listen to this bani carefully. He explains things to us lovingly.

O Farid, if on that day when my umbilical cord was cut, my throat had been cut instead,
I would not have fallen into so many troubles and undergone so many hardships.

My teeth, feet, eyes and ears have stopped working.
My body cries out, "Those whom I knew have left me!"

Farid Sahib Ji describes our condition; just like childhood doesn't remain forever, youth comes and leaves and then old age comes. He describes the condition of old age. Our teeth which used to chew even the hardest things, fall out, our luminous eyes close down and our ears don't work anymore. For how long can we hear using artificial devices? Further he says that our feet with which we used to travel all over and jump from high cliffs, even they don't work anymore. Then our body cries out, "My friends, those who were born at the same time as I was have left me." We go to one doctor and another. Can stitches heal one totally? Farid Sahib says, "My teeth, feet, eyes and ears have stopped working. My body cries out, 'Those whom I knew have left me!' Feet, eyes, teeth: they all came with me and now they have left me while I am still here." Our worldly relatives, our family upon whom we rely, how are they going to accompany us when the parts of our body, who were our companions from the beginning, don't go with us? That is why Farid Sahib tells us, "Brothers, the profit is in doing the meditation of Naam."

> *O Farid, do good to those who do evil to you; do not fill your mind with anger.*
> *Your body will not suffer from any disease, and you will obtain everything.*

Farid Sahib doesn't tell us to fight with or beat up anyone. No religion teaches us to hate others or treat others badly. All religions and religious scriptures connect us with God Almighty. All have sung songs of the unity of humanity. They all tell us that God is within all. So, if anyone is doing evil to you, Mahatmas say, don't even think evil of them, let alone do evil. Everything will fall in your lap; it means that God Almighty will come to you because he is looking for an empty place. My Gurudev Kirpal Singh Ji Maharaj used to say, "God is in search of a man, but it is difficult to become a man." He used to say, "Become a man and God will come to you without calling him."

> *O Farid, the bird is a guest in this beautiful world-garden.*
> *The morning drums are beating; get ready to leave!*

Now Farid Sahib says, "This world is a very colorful garden. Plants of different colors: white, black, brown, are planted here, but Saints and Mahatmas are also beating their drums saying, 'Dear ones, get ready for the journey ahead and always be ready for it because no one has stayed here forever.'" You know that in the garden and in the orchard, plants and trees of various kinds and colors grow. There are mango trees, rose bushes, grape vines and many others. In the morning the caretaker comes and plays his instrument so that the birds and animals will leave. However, some of the wiser birds are always waiting for that time and, even before

The Pain of Separation

the caretaker plays the instrument, they leave. They know that eventually they have to fly away. The Mahatmas who are the Beloveds of God do not get attached to the various colors of this garden of the world. They live in this garden of the world like the wiser birds. We all are like the birds of the garden. Birds have their nest here on one day and somewhere else on the next day; they are always on the run. Is our condition any better than that? We make a house at one place and then leave it. We come back and build another one somewhere else, only to leave it again.

> *O Farid, musk is released at night. Those who are sleeping do not receive it at any cost.*
> *Those whose eyes are heavy with sleep; how can they receive it?*

Now he says that God Almighty only sends his beloved children in the human body to distribute the musk of Naam among us. Those who are lazy do not get it. They only go on thinking, planning and saying, "Yes, we know there is no liberation without Naam. But we'll think about it and maybe we'll take Naam initiation after this or that work is completed." However, no one knows the plan of God Almighty. Lovingly, he says that those lazy people do not get it at any cost because our body remains here and the wealth that we are proud of doesn't go with us. Wealth belongs to us as long as our voice comes out of our throat. When our voice stops, who gives wealth to whom? Kabir Sahib says, "By collecting pennies you have accumulated millions. At the time of your death not even your undergarment will remain on you." When we die, they empty all our pockets and take away all wealth. We know and have seen this ourselves. What else do they do? Some say, "Ask him to write a will; ask him to transfer this to me." We see all this with our own eyes, but we think that it is not going to happen with us.

> *O Farid, I thought that only I was in trouble; the whole world is in trouble! When I climbed the hill and looked around, I saw this fire in each and every home.*

I Hope to See My Lord

Now this is an issue which needs much consideration and thought. Mahatmas who have struggled with their mind and have made their life know the pain through which the world is suffering. He says that he thought the pain of lust, anger, greed, attachment and egoism was bothering only him. You know that when the fire of lust rages within, it makes one blind and makes one do beastly acts. In the same way, when the fire of attachment burns, one discards all the Masters, Saints, Gurus and Pirs and runs to where one is attached. One comes back to this world only because of the bonds of attachment. So, he says, "I thought that these passions were troubling only me."

I have often said that the physical knot of these five passions: lust, anger, greed, attachment and egoism, is behind the third eye and their astral residence is in Trikuti, the second plane. When we go to the third plane and shake off the three vestures: physical, astral and causal, from our soul, then there is no trace of them. To get there we have to struggle and suffer hunger and thirst day and night. This is not a matter of talking. It is a matter of doing. So lovingly he says, "When I rose above, when I reached there, I realized, 'Oh! They have troubled the entire creation and they are the only cause of births and deaths.'" We try to become Mahatmas by talking only but we do not realize that the mind and its passions degrade us. However, they can't do anything to Mahatmas, who have conquered them and have gone beyond them. You may read the Puranas and will find many stories of those who failed when facing the passions, but you will not find even one story of a perfect Master who failed. This is because they were aware of the power of the mind and passions and they had risen above them. This is why Farid Sahib here says, "After reaching Sach Khand I came to realize that all the intellectuals and scholars were being churned in this mill (of passions)."

Shloka of Guru Arjan Dev:

O Farid, in the midst of this beautiful earth, there is a garden of thorns. Those humble beings who are blessed by their Pir, do not suffer even a scratch.

The Pain of Separation

Now Guru Arjan Dev Ji Maharaj says, "I want to tell you lovingly about the garden you talk about. Only when we free our soul from these three covers does this world seem like a bed of flowers instead of a garden of thorns. It becomes a wonderful garden. Moreover, the one who, following his Master, does the meditation of Shabd Naam and does not stain himself, he goes away unscathed." Dharam Das, a devout disciple of Kabir Sahib, had lovingly said to his Master, "O Lord, I swear to you that I don't get the desire to indulge in these five passions, these *dacoits*,[2] even in the state of dreaming." Guru Arjan Dev Ji Maharaj lovingly says, "For a little pleasure one gets sufferings for one *crore* (ten million) days. Enchanted by the pleasure of a moment he repents again and again." He says, for the sake of one second's pleasure, one suffers for one crore days. You people are educated and you can figure out how much time that is—twenty-seven thousand years. He would be a crazy person who would suffer for ages and ages just to enjoy pleasure for one second. This is why the Masters tell us that those who meet with the perfect Masters, they do the meditation of Naam and they don't get even a scratch.

Shloka of Guru Arjan Dev:

O Farid, life is blessed and beautiful, along with the beautiful body.
Only a rare few are found, who love their beloved Lord.

Now he says, "Whose body is beautiful? By seeing whose body do the souls get liberated?" He says rare are they who are in love with their Master and have become love. By loving love, we also become love.

O river, do not destroy your banks; you too will be asked to give your account.
The river flows in whatever direction the Lord orders.

Farid Sahib says, "Remove this thought of yours that no one is watching the deeds you do." God Almighty is seeing everything. When we do so

---

[2] Thief, professional criminal.

many good karmas in so many births, God Almighty writes in our destiny the meeting with him. From childhood itself we are inclined towards satsang and Naam and we stay away from bad deeds. However, if we have done bad karmas in our past births, no matter how much anyone explains to us, no matter how much anyone loves us, we still will have bad thoughts, just like the cat who dreams of mice. Bad thoughts come no matter what we do. This is why Farid Sahib says, "The river flows in whatever direction the Lord orders." We flow in the direction he orders per our own karmas. If our intellect is filled with sins, no matter how much one teaches us, we say, "No, this is written in our fate." No, it is not God Almighty that has written in anyone's destiny that they will do bad actions, it is because of their own karmas.

We have three kinds of karmas. The first is *sanchit* (accumulated) karma, the stock of which is stored in Brahm.[3] The second kind is *pralabdha* (fate) karma, which we have to pay off in this lifetime. These are the reactions of actions done in our previous lives. These karmas are set. The third kind is *kriyaman* (present) karma, those karmas that we do now in this lifetime. When Saints and Mahatmas give us the initiation of Shabd Naam, what grace do they shower on us? Because they come to shower grace on humanity, they finish the stock of our sanchit karmas. For pralabdha karmas, they install Shabd Naam within us, and doing meditation on Shabd Naam strengthens our soul and we easily pay off those karmas. For kriyaman karmas, Masters tell us to be careful and think about the consequences of our actions before doing them. If you have sown peppers, you will harvest peppers. If you sow sugar cane, you will enjoy sugar cane. Think about what you are going to do and know that you yourself will have to reap what you sow. Don't sow peppers; think before you act. This is why he says here that our intellect is affected by the karmas we have done before. If the karmas are dirty, the intellect is dirty and if the karmas are good, the intellect is good. This is why he says, "One goes wherever God directs him to go."

---

[3] Second inner spiritual plane, on top of the physical and astral planes; also known as the causal plane or Trikuti.

The Pain of Separation

O Farid, the day passes painfully; the night is spent in anguish.
The boatman stands up and shouts, "The boat is caught in the whirlpool!"

Farid Sahib says, "All one's life, since childhood, one inherited pains. One went in bad company, one stole, one plundered, one killed and finally, in order to suffer the consequences, one had to do the rounds of the police stations and courts. Thus, one's life was ruined and in the night one suffered in anguish. Not only oneself, but family members also suffered, as they had sleepless nights wondering what was going to happen in the morning." The nights are like sleeping on thorns. God Almighty has everything in his hands and he controls it, but we become the boatman of our life and cry. It is because of ego that we say, "I do this."

The river flows on and on; it loves to eat into its banks.
What can the whirlpool do to the boat, if the boatman remains alert?

Now he says that the river of life is very long and it goes on and on. Is the cycle of eighty-four lakh births so large that it will never end? The wise person standing on the bank thinks of getting into the boat only if the boatman knows how to handle the whirlpools and storms. Saints and Mahatmas always bring the boat of Shabd Naam in this world. It is not that they have come only this time and have never come before or will not come again. That is why he says, "Brothers, get on this boat to avoid the cycle of eighty-four lakh (births)." But what is our condition? As Kabir Sahib says, "One wakes up only when he gets the beating of the Angel of Death." We wake up only when we are surrounded by pain and affliction and we face death. Then the Sikhs say, "Make him hear Sukhmani Sahib," or the Hindus say, "Make him hear Bhagavad Gita," or "Light a lamp and ask him to put his attention in that light." Now you see, if a person who is dying feels thirsty and at that time goes to dig a well, how can he be successful? If we want to drink sweet water, we have to put sugar in the water. Just by saying, "sweet water, sweet water," we cannot have sweet water. We have to make an arrangement to have sugar before we can have sweet water. If we want to go into the light, why don't we manifest that light within us while we are still alive? All Masters have said that God Almighty is residing within everyone in the form of Light and Sound, but we think that by lighting a wick made of cotton placed in a lamp made of dough and then putting our attention into that light we will be liberated. No, that is not true. Kabir Sahib says, "The lamp of *Agam* (the inaccessible plane) burns without the wick and oil." That lamp of Agam is lit within everyone. In the same way Guru Ram Das Ji Maharaj says, "The light of the Naam of the Lord is going on within everyone; one gets it by following the path of the Masters." That Light is within everyone but the gurumukh Mahatmas have its darshan and make us see it also. Masters do not ask us to have blind faith. They say, "Come, do it and see."

> *O Farid, there are dozens who say they are friends; I search, but I cannot find even one.*
> *I yearn for my Beloved like a smoldering fire.*

Saints and Mahatmas, the Beloveds of God, have searched a lot. Farid Sahib searched a lot. You may read about Guru Nanak and Baba Sawan Singh Ji and how much they searched. Baba Jaimal Singh Ji searched from east to west. He finally became successful in his search because he was comparing what he found with the Gurbani. He was looking for a Mahatma who had knowledge of and practiced the Five Shabds, as mentioned in the Sikh scriptures. Regarding myself, I have often told you that there was no society or religious place where I didn't go, looking with love and faith. There was no religious place where I didn't go because I was very open-minded. I went to mosques and in the same way I loved to go to temples. I went to gurdwaras and churches with the same love. I knew since my childhood that God Almighty was everywhere. I did not hate anyone; in order to find the truth, one has to go everywhere. In the same way Farid Sahib went everywhere. He says, "It is a pity that I met many who did the talking." You will find dozens who talk. Further he says, "I didn't find even one friend of the kind that I was looking for, who was a knower of the inner secret, a meditator of the Shabd Naam who goes within." Guru Nanak Sahib says, "No one has realized him by talking." If God Almighty

The Pain of Separation

could be realized by talking alone why did the Masters have to go through so much? You see, Guru Nanak Sahib slept on beds of stones and pebbles for eleven years. Could he not get comfortable beds? He ate bushes and sand. Could he not get good food? God Almighty cannot be realized by talking. It is a matter of sacrifice. That is why Farid Sahib says that they all only talk from outside but from the within they cannot become detached.

O Farid, this body is always barking. Who can stand this constant suffering?
I have put plugs in my ears; I don't care how much the wind is blowing.

We know that those who want to meditate on Shabd Naam have to accept certain conditions and sacrifice many things. What are those things? They have to give up the pride of their position. They have to make their heart strong in order to bear the taunts and criticisms of the people. Giving up happiness, they have to call for pain. That is why he lovingly says, "When we complete these exercises, God Almighty makes us reach his palace." He gives us honor even in this world. It is not like he only gives us pain, but the way to get happiness is through pain. Gold is obtained from a mine after many difficulties. If we want to get pearls, we have to dive deep in the ocean. Masters tell us that happiness which ends in unhappiness cannot be called happiness. Up until now no one has ever got anything from indulgence in pleasure.

Once a man taunted Farid Sahib, "Your body has become emaciated; you don't even get good food to eat. You people don't get married. Even if you people do get married, you leave and go into the forest to do devotion. You are not even worth talking to. You have no honor, no name and fame." Farid Sahib smiled and told him, "This body barks every day and asks for the pleasures of lust, anger, greed, attachment and egoism, but I don't become a dog following him." Baba Bishan Das, who initiated me into the Two Words, did not eat salt or sugar for a major part of his life. When we would offer him food, he would say, "I have tied the dog and he cannot bark." Farid Sahib says the same thing here, "I have put plugs in my ears; I don't care how much the wind is blowing. I hear neither lust nor anger nor the other passions. They go away after barking; I don't listen to them."

O Farid, God's dates have ripened, and rivers of honey flow.
With each passing day, your life is being stolen away.

Someone asked Farid Sahib, "Why are you sitting here, hungry? I am going to Mecca in Arabia, the birthplace of Prophet Mohammed. Why don't you come with me?" It is a common practice among Muslims. They believe that whosoever goes to Mecca and circles around the Kaaba, his life becomes successful. However, the perfect Masters who were born in the Muslim religion do not agree with this belief. They say, "No, God is within and we cannot realize him from outside." That person asked Farid Sahib to come with him as there were many dates there which were very sweet, and he would feed him dates. Farid Sahib told him, "If you were to go within, you will find orchards laden with sweet fruits. Those dates are the sweetest." All Masters have agreed that within us we have orchards and also within us is the caretaker of those orchards. Whatever we see outside, God Almighty has put all those things within us too. Pipa Sahib says, "Whatever is in the Brahmand, the same is found within the body. He who searches for them, finds them. O Pipa, the Supreme Lord resides within and Satguru makes us see him." We should get such a Mahatma who himself goes within and can take us there. So, Farid lovingly says that the dates of almighty Lord are very sweet. Kabir Sahib says, "O Kabir, fakiri is far away, just like dates on the date tree. If one climbs the date tree, he gets the fruit of immortality; otherwise, falling down, he is broken into pieces." Just like the fruit of a date tree is very far away, so is the devotion of God. Our life is very long, and we encounter many storms and ups and downs in it. One can obtain Naam, the nectar, only if we go within by doing meditation.

O Farid, my withered body has become a skeleton; the crows are pecking at
my palms.
Even now, God has not come to help me; behold, this is the fate of all mortal
beings.

The Pain of Separation

Now lovingly he says, "My body has withered and become a skeleton; my ribs are visible but crows still bother me, they still peck at me. They ask for their food. They want me to indulge them." Farid Sahib calls the passions of lust, anger, greed, attachment and egoism the crows. You see, this is our condition. We become old but still we do not turn away from the passions. We think that no one is watching us. No, just look within yourself and see what you are doing even in your old age. What do the Masters tell us in their writings? "O Friend, indulging in the five passions, you have wasted your life. Your mind is not content even now. When will he become content? Will he be satisfied now after indulging?" This is our condition. The body has dried up and has become a skeleton, diseases have finished everything of the body, but the mind has still not withdrawn from the passions.

King Bharthari had left everything in search of God. He left his palaces, wives, wealth and everything and was going down the street. Someone had spit over there and the spit was shining in the sunlight. He thought it was a jewel and he tried to pick it up, but he only filled his hand with spit. He cursed his mind a million times, saying, "I gave up beautiful palaces, women and friends. O my mind, thinking it was a jewel, I filled my hand with spit." Once Farid Sahib saw a dog who was sick. There were worms in his body and blood was oozing out. He could hardly walk and couldn't even get up. He was hungry as no one would feed him. You know, who cares for such dogs? He saw a bitch and he went to her and started licking her with the desire to indulge with her. Farid cursed him saying, "Look at your condition. Still these passions are pecking at you." Farid Sahib says that the condition of an old man becomes like this; he still doesn't give up the passions of the world.

> *The crows have searched my skeleton and eaten all my flesh.*
> *But please do not touch these eyes; I hope to see my Lord.*

He says that these five passions have completely finished his body. Guru Nanak Sahib says, "Pleasures cause disease and one repents in the end. Thus, he comes and goes and suffers pain." We get diseases from indulging in pleasure and then we go to the doctors and beg, "Please treat me." What

I Hope to See My Lord

treatment can the doctors give? Only you can treat yourself. That is why he says that the passions have eaten up all his flesh but still, look at his bad luck; he doesn't stop and go towards God Almighty; he continues towards the passions. Further Farid begs, "O Crows, don't eat up the flesh of my body as my beloved God resides in it. I am doing devotion; I am meditating on Naam and you have no place here. Go to those who give you a place to stay."

Crow, do not peck at my skeleton; if you have landed on it, fly away.
Do not eat the flesh from that skeleton, within which my Husband Lord abides.

Lovingly he says, "O Crow, God resides within this body. My body dried up doing meditation and you have no right to eat up the skeleton, where God lives. I never used you. I am exactly the same as I had come. God is within me. Go and find some other place to stay."

O Farid, the poor grave calls out, "O homeless one, come back to your home.
You shall surely have to come to me; do not be afraid of death."

Now Farid Sahib says that the grave calls out to you. It means that when old age comes, we know that death is standing by our bedside. Still we ask our children to find some doctor and search for some means to increase our life span. However, Masters say, "Brother, what can happen then?" This is why he becomes afraid. He calls his wife and other relatives for help. One of my friends here in Rajasthan once consumed too much ginger, which created heat in his body, and he became sick. He called Gurmel and asked Gurmel to call his children. I had gone to Bombay at that time. When I returned, I was informed and so I asked him, "Could your children have saved you, if you were to die?" We always witness such incidents. Farid says that the grave is calling. It says, "Why are you afraid of death? I am your final destination."

These eyes have seen a great many leave.
O Farid, the people have their own fate, and I have mine.

The Pain of Separation

Farid Sahib says we see with our own eyes that our friends, family and companions leave us. We ourselves carry them to the cremation ground or graveyard. We either cremate them or bury them as per the rituals of our religion. Some religions also leave the body at a place where birds, vultures and other animals eat them up. Regardless, we still think that death is only for them; for us are the worldly pleasures, wines and delicious foods. He says, "These eyes have seen a great many leave." Further he says, "The people have their own fate, and I have mine." People have their own concerns and agendas. Some want their children to settle down, others want name and fame, some are struggling hard day and night to become scholars, and so forth. Everyone is worried about their own fate, but Farid is concerned for his own fate. If one realizes God Almighty, one's coming into this human body is successful. Otherwise, one's condition would be just like animals who eat and sleep and then go, or birds who eat and sleep and then fly away. One's human birth would go to waste.

> *God says, "If you reform yourself, you shall meet me, and meeting me, you shall be at peace.*
> *O Farid, if you will be mine, the whole world will be yours."*

Earlier also I said that my beloved Gurudev used to say, "God is in search of a man. He is always trying to find a man, but it is very difficult to become a man." In the same way God Almighty says, "O Farid, he who reforms himself, amends himself, I become of him. I go and set up my residence within him. If he makes me his very own, a time comes when the entire world becomes his." We know that in the Silver Age, Lord Rama came and we still remember him with much love and devotion. Does anyone remember any other king of that time with so much love and devotion? No. It has been a long time since Kabir Sahib was born. Still, not only in India but across the oceans and on top of the mountains, he is known and adored. In the same way, Guru Nanak Sahib Ji also ruled over the hearts of people. You know how every morning people get up and remember their names. Why is it so? Do we remember kings and emperors like that? No. We remember the Masters because they gave God Almighty a place to reside within them. They reformed themselves and also reformed the people around them. A satsangi has a great responsibility. If he is reformed, it is his duty to reform others. He should tell others, "Brother, by following this path I have made my life. You also do this." The fragrance of Naam should come out from the satsangi. Everyone should know where he goes. That is why God lovingly says, "If you will be mine, the whole world will be yours."

> *How long can the tree remain implanted on the riverbank?*
> *O Farid, how long can water be kept in a soft (unbaked) clay pot?*

Now Farid asks how long can a tree which is living on the riverbank survive when there is so much water there affecting its roots? What can its lifespan be? When the force of rushing water hits its roots, the sand holding it will be washed away and it will fall. Farid Sahib then says that, in the same way, our body is like an unbaked clay pot and the water (of life) is seeping through it. It is seeping through the pores of lust, anger, greed, attachment and egoism. Moreover, it has nine holes through which life is being drained out. Day and night, life is being drained out of the body. What hope do we have for its survival? How long can you keep water in an unbaked vessel? Farid Sahib says that it is beneficial only if we meditate sitting in this body. Otherwise, we leave it here, wasting the opportunity. We get the body here and leave it here.

> *O Farid, the mansions are vacant; those who lived in them have gone to live underground.*
> *They remain there, in those honorless graves.*

Even now we can see the ruins of the forts and palaces. Even though the authorities preserve them for the sake of history, we often find only their foundations. Everyone has his own angle of vision. When I went to Delhi in 1947, while I was in the Army, we were shown the Red Fort. The guide told us the entire history of that fort and of the kings who lived there. He showed us the Diwan-i-khas (Private Royal Chamber), the Diwan-i-aam

The Pain of Separation

(General Assembly Chamber), the Nahr-i-bihisht (Heavenly Canal) and the private baths, etc. He showed us the places where Shah Jahan, who had built that fort, used to sit, eat and sleep. He showed us how convenient his bathrooms were, equipped with both hot and cold water even in those times. After telling us the whole story, he told us that Shah Jahan was imprisoned by his own son Aurangzeb and he died in the fort of Agra. Many people go to see those places and they all have their own understanding and angle of vision. I came down with fever when I heard the whole story. I thought, "What kind of karmas did Shah Jahan have? He spent so much to create the luxurious palaces and then enjoy them. For his son, he had done so much, spent so much and donated so much, first to celebrate his birth and then, later on, for his upbringing. However, he would have never imagined that the same son would imprison him. It is written in his history that Shah Jahan wrote a letter to his son saying, "Dear son, the Hindus whom you hate even try to send food for their dead parents in the heavens and they do a lot of charity in their name. I am your father and am still alive. At least ask the guard, whom you have appointed to guard me, to give me enough water to drink." Aurangzeb replied, "Drink the ink with which you have written the letter when you feel thirsty." You can very well imagine: a king was deprived even of water.

The palaces are empty now. Pigeons live there and the feces of the pigeons is not cleaned up. Is there anyone to clean those places? No. On the other side of the same city of Delhi, there is the place where, by the orders of the same king Aurangzeb, the authorities killed Guru Tegh Bahadur Ji. People go there with so much respect that they don't even carry their shoes in there. All day long they distribute *parshad*[4] and sing his praises there. You can see yourself how that Fakir is being honored even after so much time, and how people are bowing their heads to that place. If Aurangzeb had known that this Mahatma would be honored and respected so much, while people would curse Aurangzeb himself, he would not have killed Guru Tegh Bahadur Ji. There was no fort where Guru Tegh Bahadur was killed but now

---

[4] Food blessed by a Saint, given as a way of bestowing grace.

I Hope to See My Lord

that place is covered with gold, whereas the fort where Aurangzeb lived, no one is even there to clean it. That is why the Masters say, "Palaces become empty and animals live there. Souls go to their graves and suffer curses."

O Sheikh, dedicate yourself to God; you will have to depart, today or tomorrow.

O Farid, the shore of death looks like the river-bank, being eroded away. Beyond is the burning hell, from which cries and shrieks are heard.

Farid Sahib says death comes with such a force. It is just like the force of water that gushes towards the dam and breaks it. Further he says that over there are the cauldrons with heated oil in which the Angels of Death are deep-frying the jivas. The sounds which come from there are like the ones coming from the battlefield, "Kill him, get him, throw him in the oil." The Angels of Death tell the jivas, "You have done this bad deed or committed that torture and now you are to suffer." This is the condition over there.

Some understand this completely, while others wander around carelessly.

He says that some get the understanding and they do the meditation of Naam, live up to the satsang, and accept whatever the Masters said. Others wander carelessly. They say, "Oh, we'll see later. Who is going to ask for the accounts? This world is sweet, who has seen the beyond?" Dear ones, it is easy to say things like that but such thoughts are misleading. Even in this world you see that not everyone in the same village or same family shares the same kind of fate. Some are affluent, some are poor, some are paying off through sickness, some suffer becoming jobless. When we see that not everyone is equal here, how can we say that in the court of the Lord no one will ask for the accounts and decide our fate accordingly? Guru Nanak Dev Ji Maharaj says, "O Nanak, after creating the jivas, he made the Lord of Judgment judge them. Over there only the true ones are accepted. The false ones are removed and kept separately. The false ones do not find a place there. Their faces are

The Pain of Separation

blackened and they go to the hells." He says that the false (dirty) souls do not get any place there.

> *Those actions which are done in this world, shall be examined in the court of the Lord.*

He says that God Almighty or the Lord of Judgment doesn't need any witnesses or arguments. Your deeds, good or bad, will themselves bear witness.

> *O Farid, the crane perches on the riverbank, playing joyfully.*
> *While it is playing, a hawk suddenly pounces on it.*
> *When the hawk of God attacks, playful sport is forgotten.*
> *God does what is not expected or even considered.*

Farid Sahib makes us understand by giving an outward example. He says that a crane is sitting on the bank of a river. We know that the crane is a beautiful creature. He is standing on one leg and is in deep concentration. Although it may seem that he is concentrating on God, he is not; he is concentrating on and remembering frogs and fish. When he finds a fish, he catches it and throws it up in the air and when it comes down, he catches it again. He is playing with them like this and is happy enjoying the game. Then a hawk attacks that crane who is enjoying his game. Hawks are also created in the will of God and their food is also other creatures. When the hawk pounces on the crane, the crane forgets the game he was playing with the fish. In the same way, we are playing the games of enjoying pleasures, drinking wine, and so forth in the wonderful garden of this world. We are killing other creatures, marinating and spicing them, and then eating them. We say that goats, sheep, hens and cows, etc., are created for our food. Just consider this: if someone who is stronger than us kills us, deep-fries us, eats us and then says, "You are created for us," what would we feel? Happiness or pain? Think about this patiently; if someone kills our child in our presence, would it not bring tears in our eyes? Of course, we would cry and we would complain. Just imagine the mothers when, right

I Hope to See My Lord

in front of them, we snatch away their children; we take away calves from cows and lambs from sheep. They also shed tears, but who listens to their complaints? Is there any court in this world where they can file their petitions? A hunter shoots an arrow or shoots a rifle and injures a deer or a rabbit. Does anyone tend to their wounds? They somehow hide and save their lives, but the hunters still track them down. It is possible that in the past those creatures were better human beings than us. They may have been very wealthy or renowned people, but since they made mistakes in their human birth, they have come back into the forms of lower creatures and are paying off their accounts. Now when we are making those same mistakes, is it not possible that we may come back like they have, in order to settle our accounts? Guru Nanak Sahib says, "No one is spared from settling accounts."

One time a lion was killing a goat and the goat laughed. The lion said, "It is surprising that you are laughing. Are you not feeling pain?" She said, "Of course I feel pain. It is not that I don't feel pain; everyone loves life. However, I am laughing because we, the goats, are creatures who eat leaves and bushes and yet we are deskinned and killed. If someone would listen, I want to pray that they should make our progeny impotent, so that they would never bear any children to face this situation. I am laughing because I am wondering what will be your fate, you who are killing us harmless creatures."

Kabir Sahib says, "The goat eats leaves and is deskinned. What will be the condition of those who eat goats?" He whose meat we are deep-frying today, will certainly do the same to us later. God Almighty has not given this concession to anyone that in every life one can cut, marinate, spice and deep-fry the flesh of others for his consumption and then not have to pay for it. That is why he says that, like the hawk made the crane forget all the games he was playing at the riverbank, in the same way, when the hawk of death pounces upon us, we forget all the pleasures we have enjoyed. Brothers, all the dining and wining is forgotten. I have seen many people who tremble when the Angel of Death arrives. Then they say, "We have committed many sins, no one is worse than us. When will God forgive us?" They should have repented earlier. Masters tell us, "When the

The Pain of Separation

hawk of God attacks, playful sport is forgotten. God does what is not expected or even considered." It means that he who kills and eats others, and plays with others' lives, does he consider or expect that death will come to him? No, he thinks that death is not for him. It is for others. Saints and Mahatmas, whose inner eyes are opened, tell us that just like a human being has the right to live on this earth, birds and animals also have the same right to live. Masters tell us, "Treat your neighbors the way you would like to be treated."

> *The body is of three and a half maund[5] and runs on water and grain.*
> *The mortal comes into the world with very little capital.*

Farid Sahib says that in this age the average weight of a body is three and a half maund (one hundred and seventy-five pounds). It runs on water and grain, but only a very small capital of breaths is given to him. They say the oldest age is one hundred years, but very few people reach the mark of one hundred years. Most of us live up to sixty or seventy years or even less, say forty to fifty years, and then we finish our journey in this world. How long can this body which runs on water and grain function? We have been sent to this world with a very small capital of breaths.

> *But when the Messengers of Death come, breaking down all the doors,*
> *They bind and gag the mortal, before the eyes of his beloved brothers.*
> *Behold, the mortal being is going away, carried on the shoulders of four men.*

Farid Sahib says, "Look here, O Dear One, when death comes all the members of the family are present there, but no one among them is thinking about what the dying person is going through or if there was any way to save him from the death. When he is dead, they put him on a coffin and tie him up so tight that he cannot roll over and fall off." Once I saw that an old woman died and, before taking her for cremation, all the grandchildren

---

[5] A *maund* is a unit of weight in Asia, equal to fifty pounds.

were asked to come and pay their last respects to her by touching her feet. People do such things all the time. One of her daughters-in-law did not allow her son to touch the dead woman's feet. She said that he had gotten a blessed talisman and if he were to touch the dead body, the old woman might stick to him as a ghost and he would lose the blessed effect of the talisman. So, Farid Sahib says, "They bind and gag the mortal, before the eyes of his beloved brothers." We used to be so proud of our brothers and family members and look what happens to them; people tie their corpses down onto the bier with ropes. "Behold, the mortal being is going away, carried on the shoulders of four men…. Only those good deeds done in the world will be of any use in the court of the Lord." Only our actions done in this world are useful; none of our family members protect us or help us after death. They cannot do anything. You see, the members of our family are sitting there and no one knows from what direction the Angel of Death will come and, holding its ears, take the dying soul. What help can they give us? Kabir Sahib says, "The drums are being beaten, the army is standing on guard, but the Angel of Death comes into the room and takes the soul."

One cannot go to the cremation ground himself. Farid says, "Behold, the mortal being is going away, carried on the shoulders of four men."

O Farid, only those good deeds done in the world will be of any use in the court of the Lord.
O Farid, I am a sacrifice to those birds which live in the jungle.
They peck at the roots and live on the ground, but they do not leave the Lord's side.

Farid Sahib says, "I am a sacrifice to those birds which live in the jungle." In this world we also live like those birds. He says that he sacrifices himself on those Mahatmas who eat fruits, leaves and simple things to survive, because they do not crave for and get attached to eating delicious foods. There is a story from our Satguru Sawan Singh Ji's life. Bhai Banta Singh, who was his cook, himself used to say that many times he would put salt into Master Sawan's food when he was supposed to put sugar. One

The Pain of Separation

time, Baba Sawan Singh Ji had called for some food and Bhai Banta Singh thought of making a recipe using sugar. However, by mistake he put in salt instead. Master didn't complain. When Bhai Banta Singh later tasted that food himself, he realized his mistake. He went to the Master and said, "Master, I put salt into your food instead of sugar." Master smiled and said, "Masters never taste the foods. While eating, they take their attention within. One can know the taste of food only if attention is at the tongue." That is why here he says that he sacrifices on those Mahatmas who do their meditation after eating whatever simple food they get, but they do not leave the Lord's side.

> *O Farid, the seasons change, the woods shake and the leaves drop from the trees.*
> *I have searched in the four directions, but I have not found any resting place anywhere.*

Now he says the seasons change, woods shake and the old leaves fall down. Spring goes away and autumn comes. The leaves that fall down do not go back to the trees; they just go on blowing from one place to another. Who can put them back on the branches from which they fell? The same is our condition. Old age comes and the organs of this body refuse to function. Nowadays even the heads of young people wobble, trembling and moving due to weakness, but in old age the head wobbles like a steering wheel wobbles when the wheels are not aligned. The hands tremble and the feet shake. What one says doesn't make sense. He puts a morsel in his mouth but it goes somewhere else, so the family members have to feed him. What are we proud of? Who knows what is going to happen with us? One goes from one doctor to another and prays to them to save him or at least cure his wobbling. But how can that be done? It is like the story of fallen leaves, which sometimes blow to one place and sometimes to another.

> *O Farid, I have torn my clothes to tatters; now I wear only a rough blanket.*
> *Let me wear only those clothes which will lead me to meet my Lord.*

I Hope to See My Lord

At the time when Farid Sahib came, the dress of the fakirs was normally a blanket, usually a black one. That is why fakirs were called "the ones who wear the black blanket." In the beginning, Farid Sahib used to wear normal clothes because he knew that just by taking up the outer appearance of the fakirs one's mind doesn't come under control. That is why Farid Sahib says, "I have torn my clothes to tatters; now I wear only a rough blanket. Let me wear only those clothes which will lead me to meet my Lord."

Shloka of Guru Amar Das:

Why do you tear apart your fine clothes, and take to wearing a rough blanket?
O Nanak, even sitting in your own home, you can meet the Lord, if your
  mind is in the right place.

Whenever the Masters come in this world, they never preach that by wearing white clothes instead of saffron-colored clothes you will meet God Almighty. They also never preach that by giving up saffron-colored clothes and wearing black clothes you will realize him. It would be very easy if we could realize God Almighty only by wearing clothes of a certain color. Masters tell us, "Remain in your own religion. Remain in your own household. Attend to the responsibilities you have been given and do the meditation of Shabd Naam." However, coming here, we all forget because our implacable enemy, the mind, is sitting within us. He creates various thoughts within us. Sometimes he surrounds us with waves of lust, anger and attachment. Sometimes he tells us, "Give up your home and become a sadhu, a fakir." When one leaves his home and becomes a sadhu, he tells him, "Go back home. There is nothing here. You can do the devotion even at home." The mind doesn't let us be able to live a householder's nor a renunciate's life. That is why here he says, "Dear one, what is the use of tearing your clothes? What is the need for leaving your home? If you do the meditation of Shabd Naam you can realize God Almighty, even sitting at home."

About three hundred years ago the yogis who wore saffron-colored robes were very prominent. Even as recently as thirty to forty years ago there were many yogis like them. We used to think that they had met with

The Pain of Separation

God by wearing those colored robes. Guru Gobind Singh Ji Maharaj used to practice and preach Shabd Naam. He neither condemned nor endorsed any particular outer garb. However, when his disciples started believing that only by adopting a certain outer garment one could meet God, he put the skin of a tiger on a donkey and let him roam free outside of the fort. He did not tell anyone that he had done this. Next morning, when people went out of the fort, they saw the donkey with the tiger skin on it. They got scared and ran back into the fort, saying, "Master, there is a tiger wandering outside!" Guru Gobind Singh Ji replied, "Okay, I'll make some arrangement to take care of this." This went on for a few days. When Guru Gobind Singh Ji saw that in their minds the people believed that there was a tiger outside the fort, he took some of his brave warriors with him, opened the door of the fort and left the open door unattended. The donkey ran inside the fort and when he saw his donkey brethren carrying the bricks of a potter, he brayed aloud. The potter recognized the donkey as one of his own donkeys. He wondered why the donkey was wearing the skin of a tiger and what he was up to. He removed the tiger skin from the donkey and loaded bricks on him. The people who used to say to Guru Gobind Singh Ji that a tiger had come to kill them, etc., became embarrassed. Guru Sahib said, "Dear ones, I created this drama to make you understand that by putting on the skin of a tiger, a donkey cannot become a tiger. How can one become a Mahatma by wearing colored robes?"

It is said, "You have taken up this appearance to intimidate people. To eat without working for it, you have called yourself 'Baba.'" It is only for scaring people that we take up such garbs. We stop earning our livelihood and start living off others' earnings. Kabir Sahib says, "O Kabir, the food of a householder is very bad—its teeth measure nine inches. One can survive it if he (the recipient) meditates. Otherwise it rips out his ribs." No one feeds others free of charge. This is my personal experience; I have seen this myself that when the *bhai*, the priest of the gurdwara, comes to ask for food, the lady circles the chapatis around her sick son's head and gives them to him. Now you think about this: will he not be affected who eats such food, food that he has not earned himself? It definitely will have an effect. This is why, whenever Saints and Mahatmas come into this world, they earn their livelihood by the sweat of their brow. They tell us to also earn our livelihood honestly and feed our children with those earnings. "The kind of food we eat makes our mind like that." If you feed your children with food obtained through dishonest means, it will have a very bad effect on them. They will never obey you. How can they be good if you have not reared them properly? I have seen many government employees who accept bribes and make nice homes, etc., but when their children grow up, the children don't respect them. Those people come to me and boast of the good upbringing and the education they gave to their children, but then complain that still their children don't respect them. Most of the time I keep quiet, but when someone wants to hear the reason for their problem, I make them understand. I ask them, "Dear one, did you spare anyone? What kind of earnings have you spent on your children?"

Tulsi Sahib says, "Give up eating other people's earnings. Otherwise you will have to come back to repay them." Go through the lives of the perfect Masters and you will find that they all earned their livelihood by the sweat of their brow. Kabir Sahib said, "I would die but never beg for my body." He said he would never stretch out his hands in front of anyone, even if he died by not doing so. Read the life of our Satguru Ji Maharaj, who earned his livelihood by sweat of his brow. Kabir Sahib wove on the loom all his life. Guru Nanak Sahib did farming in the village of Kartarpur. He maintained himself and his children with those earnings. He said, "Never bow down to one who calls himself Guru or Pir and still goes begging. Nanak says, he who works for his livelihood and shares with others, knows the path to God." For whom will God Almighty open his door? Only for him who earns his livelihood by the sweat of his brow and who also serves the Sadhu and the sangat out of those earnings. Masters come as an example in this world. They do it themselves and tell their disciples, "Do this and only then will God open his door." You can deceive people, but you cannot deceive God Almighty who resides within you.

Take this thought out of your mind that if a few people, or if five or ten thousand people, call you a Mahatma, you become one. I have always said that those who are illiterate here, they will be illiterate in the way ahead too. In the same way, God Almighty will not award the degree of Mahatma

The Pain of Separation

after death to those who are thieves and dacoits and who usurp other people's things. That is why one should earn one's livelihood honestly. Guru Amar Das Sahib explained to us, "Even sitting in your own home, you can meet the Lord, if your mind is in the right place." Brother, if you keep your mind at the right place and clean your inner self then you don't need to go to the forests or the top of the mountains; even in your home you can meet God Almighty. It is only by doing the meditation of Shabd Naam that one can clean his within.

We should lay emphasis on understanding the writings of Saints and Mahatmas. None of their writings tell us to go on reading day and night like a parrot without understanding what we are reading. Masters tell us to read the scriptures, as without reading we cannot get awareness. However, we should understand what we read and understand what the bani is telling us. Guru Nanak Sahib tells us, "He who owns this house has locked it up and we can get the key from the Master. Unless we take refuge in the Satguru, we cannot get it by taking numerous measures." God Almighty, who has made this body, has handed the key to unlock it over to the gurumukhs. No Saint or Mahatma tells us a new thing. Every Mahatma has given the message of Shabd Naam and has preached Shabd Naam. We should take advantage of this human body; who knows whether we will get it again or not? Kabir Sahib says, "Human birth is precious. It doesn't happen again and again. It is just like ripened fruit; once it falls off it doesn't go back to the branch of the tree."

Chapter 7

Let Patience Become Your Nature

Saints and Mahatmas, the Beloveds of God, always come into this world. Their path has never been closed, nor can it be closed. Numerous Mahatmas have come into this world, and many more have yet to come. All Masters have told us that there is only one God and the way to meet him is also only one. Whether one lives in the East or West, God Almighty has created each and every one and he is sitting within them all in the form of Shabd. Masters have also told us that God Almighty is the All Owner; he doesn't have any equal, brother or friend. To whom does he show the path? To whom does he explain the way and the process by which we can meet him? Masters put those souls on the path who have yearning to meet God. They tell those souls about the ornaments which please God Almighty and which rites and rituals he accepts. The thing that pleases God Almighty is humility or meekness. Our Hazur Satguru Kirpal used to say that God Almighty likes humility and meekness as he is the all owner. In front of whom can he bow down? If someone can adorn himself with humility, that is the greatest ornament. Only that humility which we have within is useful; it should not be for public show.

The bani of Farid Sahib is presented to you. He explains what those who are full of egoism and pride are like. They are like a high cliff or tall hill of sand where rainwater doesn't stay; it flows down off of them. Regarding those who are proud of their wealth or position and

The Pain of Separation

who crush people under their feet in the intoxication of their power, Farid Sahib says that they go from this world empty-handed just like a hill of sand remains without water; it rains but water flows down off it. Guru Nanak Sahib says, "The Lord doesn't like egoism, even the Vedas say this." He says, "Read the Vedas and Shastras and other scriptures and you will know that God Almighty doesn't accept egoism. He only accepts humility." People take pride in the big families they have, the many strong brothers they have, the wealth they have and the strong body they have, but they come into this world empty-handed and leave it empty-handed. In the world beyond, no one from our community, nor our brothers and sisters, can help us. Farid Sahib asks, "What are you proud of?" Are you proud of your health? When we get fever, in a few days our face becomes yellow and becomes like a frog. Are we proud of our youth? Have we not seen anyone's old age? Are we proud of our wealth? Have we not seen poor people begging on the streets? Are we proud of our community? Have we not seen that when we take our friends to the cremation ground, no matter how loud we cry and mourn and no matter how many of us go there, still we cannot do any good to the departed ones? Those who die go away and never return to this world; only memories are left. So, Masters say, what are you proud of? God Almighty loves only humility.

Shloka of Guru Arjan Dev:

O Farid, those who are very proud of their greatness, wealth and youth,
Will return empty-handed from this world, like sand hills after the rain.

Mahmud Ghaznavi invaded India seventeen or eighteen times and plundered a lot of gold and silver. There was a time when India used to be called "the Golden Sparrow," but people like Mahmud Ghaznavi invaded from outside and snatched away its wings. No country has been poor in all times and no country remains rich forever. It is possible that countries which are currently poor used to be affluent in the past, and that those which are rich now may become dependent on others and poor in the future. At the time of his death, Mahmud Ghaznavi asked his servants to lay out all the riches he had plundered. He wanted to see how much he had from the wealth that he gained by killing others and making millions of women widows and millions of children orphans. He also wanted to see how much would go with him. At the end, he told his servants, "Put my hands outside my coffin and raise a banner with this slogan: 'His hands are empty and only the tortures that he did are accompanying him.' I'll suffer for what I have done, because one who does bad things pays for it. At least my people should know that when I left, I went empty-handed."

> *O Farid, the faces of those who forget the Naam are dreadful.*
> *They suffer terrible pain here, and hereafter they find no place of rest or refuge.*

Now Farid Sahib lovingly says, "Whose faces are not worth beholding? Whose faces are dreadful? Those who, in this human body, have forgotten God Almighty and have given up simran." They don't get any happiness in this world. Sometimes they are trapped in the passions. Sometimes they are stuck in fights and war. Sometimes they drown in waves of lust and anger. We lose our peace in all these things. That is why Kabir Sahib said, "Be afraid of those who have been kept away from the devotion of the Lord." Whom should we fear in this world? We should fear those who have gone away from the devotion of the Lord and who do not believe in the existence of God Almighty. Love the devotees of God because they see him within all and understand them as the Lord himself. Saints always look at the soul and they understand that the evil is in our mind. Guru Nanak Dev Ji Maharaj says, "I have seen the shameless people without Naam rub their noses (in repentance) and their noses are cut." He says that he has seen that, in the court of the Lord, Kal punishes them. Kal tells them, "You were given a precious human birth to do the work you could not do in the bodies of birds and animals. That is the devotion of Naam and you did not do it." Kabir Sahib says, 'The day is lost playing, the night is lost in sleep. Birth was as precious as a jewel but was wasted like shells."

The Pain of Separation

O Farid, if you do not awaken in the early hours before dawn, you are dead while yet alive.
Although you have forgotten God, God has not forgotten you.

Farid Sahib says, "Don't understand him as alive who, after getting the human birth, does not wake up in the early hours and meditate. There is no difference between him and the dead ones." What do the Beloveds of God say? Guru Arjan Dev Ji Maharaj writes in his bani, "O Night, may you increase as I am in love with my Beloved. O Sleep, may you decrease as I am with my Lord." Guru Nanak Ji says, "When the sun rises, birds praise the Lord and numerous colors are spread. Saints create amazing forms, says Nanak, with the colors of Naam." Upon sunrise, birds praise the Lord in their own language. By that time the Beloveds of the Lord have already made their union with him, whereas the worldly people are sleeping in the intoxication of maya. That is why he says that those who do not stay awake in the early hours doing the devotion are not alive. One should understand them as dead. We have been given this human birth after going through the cycle of eighty-four lakhs of births. If we do not finally do simran and make our union with God Almighty, who knows how long we will be asleep in the grave, where no one will wake us up.

Shloka of Guru Arjan Dev:

O Farid, my Husband Lord is full of joy; he is great and self-sufficient.
To be imbued with the Lord God, this is the most beautiful decoration.

Farid Sahib says that the omnipotent, omnipresent God Almighty is not dependent on anyone. He is self-sufficient. What does he accept? He accepts union with him. Those Beloveds of God, those children of God, who make their union with him, that union becomes their spiritual practice, their rites and rituals and their decoration. This is what he likes and accepts. He wants us to vacate the nine openings of the body, rise above, do the devotion and become one with him. Those who do that become one with God, just like sugar is in the candy.

Let Patience Become Your Nature

Shloka of Guru Arjan Dev:

O Farid, look upon pleasure and pain as the same; eradicate corruption from your heart.
Whatever pleases the Lord God is good; understand this, and then you will find his court.

We are not the body. We are the soul. We have got the body to pay off our karmas. Guru Nanak Sahib says, "Do not get excited seeing happiness, do not weep seeing pains. Happiness and pains are alike, they come as it is ordained by the Lord." He says not to get afraid looking at pains; have patience. Don't get excited seeing happiness and don't boast of your wisdom. Do you think you have got happiness due to your own efforts? He says, "No, it is not like that." When pain comes, it is due to our karma. If we get happiness, even that is due to our karma. He says that God Almighty opens his door to those who understand both pain and happiness as the same and who clean their hearts. They understand that everything comes from God and is in his will. Birth and death happen in his will. Not a leaf can turn without his will. Why do we jivas feel bothered in this suffering world? We become the doer of everything. We don't thank God when happiness comes because we say that it has come because of our own wisdom and efforts. You see, we have the same wisdom and make the same efforts when difficulties come in our life. In those times we find fault with God and we leave him. We stop believing in him and we say, "Where is God?"

There was an old woman who became very sick and her family members felt that it would be helpful if she would do the devotion of the Lord. They told her, "You are so sick that you cannot even move yourself. You can't even go to the toilet yourself, and no one else can help you. At least now you should remember him and he will help you." She got upset at them and said, "It is God who has given me so much pain and disease, and you are asking me to do his devotion?" How can God Almighty open his door to such people?

The Pain of Separation

Shloka of Guru Arjan Dev:

O Farid, the world dances as it dances, and you dance with it as well.
Only that soul does not dance with it who is under the care of the Lord God.

Farid Sahib says that people dance like others dance. We do things like others do. We imitate others. We say, "Let me also do what he does. He has indulged in lust, let me do it also. He is meditating on Naam, let me meditate also." We do not do anything from our heart. We don't have the spirit of doing things ourselves. We don't have the enthusiasm to do it ourselves; we always follow others. Farid says, "O Farid, the world dances as it dances, and you dance with it as well." He says, "It is a pity and I am sorry to say that even though you are called a devotee, O Farid, you also dance like them! You are also stuck in rites and rituals like others and you also follow the path which others are treading upon." Further he says, "But it has come in my understanding that he who is under the care of Allah (God Almighty) does not dance like others." He does not follow the path of the worldly people by looking at them. Worldly people walk like sheep. One follows the other and they have no awareness of spirituality. Master Sawan Singh Ji used to say, "One sheep goes into the ditch and the others follow him there. The barn is on fire and the shepherds mercifully try to save them by directing them away from the fire, but they cannot give up the company of the other sheep. If one goes towards the fire, they all go after him." However, he who is under the care of God Almighty and who is involved in doing devotion does not dance in the world like the others.

Shloka of Guru Arjan Dev:

O Farid, the heart is attached with this world, but the world is of no use to it at all.
It is so difficult to get the company of the Fakirs, the holy Saints; it is only achieved by perfect karma.

Let Patience Become Your Nature

Farid Sahib says that the heart is engrossed in the world, but think about it patiently: is there anything of this world which will be useful to you? The things of the world, which we have become so bothered about, will not go with us. He says that only those who have very good karma get the company of Fakirs, the satsangs of the Master Saints. If we do not have good karma, we will sleep in satsang or go back finding fault with the Master, saying, "He doesn't know how to talk. I am more learned than him. I can speak better than him." Normally, when a learned Master is giving a talk, we say, "He is a great philosopher, he speaks very well." Rare are the fortunate ones who understand the real meaning of satsang and understand the grace that Masters shower upon the jivas. Rare are those who pay attention to the nectar which the Masters are sprinkling upon them in the satsang through their words. Fortunate are those who receive their share of nectar. Guru Amar Das Ji Maharaj says, "Master is a pot of nectar, and the rain of nectar showers there." He says that the Master is a pot of nectar, and nectar comes out from his mouth. Whatever he says, it is only for the benefit of the jivas.

The bani says, "It is only achieved by perfect karma." We can obtain it only if we have perfect karma. There are ones whose karma is perfect, and they come to satsang. They take the words of the Master as divine, but there are other jivas who, finding fault with the Masters, go away from satsang. Kabir Sahib says, "Some come with love, some without. Saints love them both without looking at their love or hatred." One takes advantage of the Masters. He who believes in and follows the Master will benefit, but if one doesn't follow the Master? "What can the poor Master do when disciples lack love and faith. They are blind and are like hollow bamboo, in which air doesn't stay." Those who get the elixir of satsang do not leave and do not care for the world.

The first watch of the night brings flowers, and the later watches of the night bring fruit.
Those who remain awake and aware, receive the gifts from the Lord.

The Pain of Separation

First, flowers come on plants or fruit trees, whether it is apple, orange, etc., and then comes fruit. Just like that, meditation done in the earlier part of the night is like flowers and meditation done in the later part is like fruit. Don't think that meditation done in the evening or any other time is a waste. Even one second spent in the devotion of Lord is counted. Baba Jaimal Singh Ji used to say that when a jiva, withdrawing his attention from all outside things, listens to the Shabd, his attendance is marked in Sach Khand. Masters whose inner eyes are opened tell us that, when any jiva sits in meditation, even gods in the heavens look at him and say in surprise, "Ah! In the Iron Age a jiva is sitting in meditation and is preparing to meet with the Lord!" The later part of the night is important because, getting up early at three a.m., we have just woken up and our surat or attention has just entered the body. We don't remember the thoughts of the previous day and there is no noise in the streets, etc. At that time, it becomes easier to withdraw the surat, the soul, from every single cell of the body, and so we get the fruit. "Those who remain awake and aware, receive the gifts from the Lord."

Once a satsangi fell at the feet of Baba Sawan Singh Ji, when he was walking, and he became very upset. We people don't realize that Masters always are connected within and if someone suddenly falls at their feet, there is a danger that they may fall down. There was another person there who said, "Maharaj Ji, please shower grace." Master Sawan Singh Ji said, "There is a time for grace. I go to every satsangi carrying a basket of grace, every morning at three a.m. Those who are awake at that time receive it. For those who are asleep, I stand for a while and then come back."

The gifts are from our Lord and Master; what will go with them?
Some are awake, and do not receive them, while he awakens others from sleep
and gives them.

Now he lovingly says the world forgets the Giver, does the devotion of the gifts and loves the gifts. However, think patiently; what will they take along with them? "The gifts are from our Lord and Master; what will go with them?" Is there anything out of these gifts that they will take with them?

Let Patience Become Your Nature

"Some are awake and do not receive them, while he awakens others from sleep and gives them." Some do not receive while they are awake, and others get them though they are sleeping. Baba Jaimal Singh Ji used to say that if we are searching for him, if we have not yet met with the Master but have yearning in our heart, even that is counted as devotion. If we are searching, Master Kirpal used to say, "There is food for the hungry and water for the thirsty." God Almighty surely makes arrangements for our meeting with the Master. You know how Baba Sawan Singh Ji blessed Master Kirpal Singh Ji with his inner darshan for seven years before he had seen Master Sawan Singh in his physical form. Is that not an example where "He woke him up and gave him gifts"? Likewise, there was a time when Baba Sawan Singh Ji had not yet met with Baba Jaimal Singh Ji. The distance between Baba Jaimal Singh's ashram and the Murree Hills, where Baba Sawan Singh Ji was working, was five to six hundred kilometers. You see how Baba Jaimal Singh went so far and found Baba Sawan Singh to give him the gift. At that time Baba Jaimal Singh Ji walked past Baba Sawan Singh, who thought, "Maybe this old man has come to the commissioner's office to resolve some pension affair." At that time Baba Jaimal Singh Ji told Bibi Rukko, "I have come here for this *sardar* (Sikh gentleman)." She said, "But he didn't even greet you. He didn't even say 'Sat Sri Akal' or 'Ram, Ram.'" He said, "What does he know? He will come to our satsang on the fourth day. Swami Ji wants to get work done by him. He doesn't know what lies in his fate." On exactly the fourth day, Baba Sawan Singh came to the satsang of Baba Jaimal Singh. When he heard Baba Jaimal Singh Ji's satsang, his doubts, which had been bothering him for twenty-two years, disappeared. He bowed his head, asking for Naam initiation, and Baba Jaimal Singh Ji blessed him. The same was this poor soul's condition. I did not meet with anyone who praised Master Kirpal nor with anyone who criticized him. You can see what a miracle it was that a Master sent his representative to me with the message, "Stay home, I am coming to see you." Is this not a surprising thing? I didn't even know Master Kirpal Singh and the person who brought the message called him "Master." It is very difficult to take a human being as a Master because, as a human being, he is involved in activities like us. However, you know the background of my life and how

The Pain of Separation

for many years I had been sitting in his remembrance. Even though I had not received the Naam, from my childhood I was not aware of anything during day or night except the remembrance of God and I would stay up all night in that remembrance.

I will tell you about one incident of my life, which is quite humorous but also provides a lesson. There was a person who used to visit me every night from eight to ten p.m. One night, before he came, I was lying on my bed, thinking that one day I would be dead. I was thinking how people would be sitting surrounding me and I wouldn't even be able to move my head or my hands. I was lying down, lost in those thoughts, when that person came in. Usually, when he would come, I would greet him, welcome him and lovingly offer him a seat, but on that day I neither said nor did anything. I wasn't even aware that he had come. Finally, he said, "What's wrong? You are not saying anything. Are you asleep?" When I heard him say that I became aware that he was there and I said, "Brother, I was not sleeping, although I was dead like Sheikh Chilli." (Sheikh Chilli was a person who used to fantasize a lot, assume that he had gotten what he was fantasizing about and then react to it.) Now you can very well imagine what kind of yearning was there which created such thoughts within a young boy. Master Kirpal accepted this yearning and he came. Furthermore, consider if a person understands someone as God, yet doesn't even ask him, "What is your caste? Are you a renunciate or a householder? Where do you live?" As I have often said, I never asked those questions of my Master. Whatever path he gave out, I did it honestly. That is why I thank him; he woke this sleeping one and made me do his devotion.

> *You search for your Husband Lord; you must have some fault in your body.*
> *Those who are known as married do not look to others.*

Someone came to Farid Sahib and asked him, "Master, we don't see God. We sit and we search for him. We try to walk on the way and we do not sin. We do all the good things. Why then do we not meet God?" Farid Sahib told him, "Dear one, the loyal married woman doesn't look at other men. She doesn't desire to receive things from others. If her husband doesn't

Let Patience Become Your Nature

have anything to give, still she is satisfied. If her husband is living in the jungle, still she is happy serving him. Such a married woman does not crave anything from anyone except from her husband. In the same way, he who does the devotion of the Master does not look to any god or goddess for help. If he is in pain or in happiness, he devotes himself only to his Master so that the karmas are paid off quickly." That is why he says, "Dear one, you have not yet become a married soul. A married soul does not desire anything. Those disciples who become devotees of the Master do not desire anything except the Master." Only with the grace of Master Kirpal Singh was I was able to utter these words: "I have not seen God; I have not seen any Khuda or Rahim. I have seen only you; I have faith only in you." It was only his grace that a jiva could have such faith in someone he had never met before.

Within yourself, make patience the bow, and make patience the bowstring.
Make patience the arrow; the Creator will not let you miss the target.

Now Farid Sahib explains, "Make a bow of patience and let your patience be the bowstring. In this way, when you shoot an arrow, it will not miss the target." When one does the devotion of God Almighty with patience and contentment, whatever words come out of such a devotee, God Almighty listens to them. Guru Nanak Sahib says, "Whatever a gurumukh speaks is heard. What a manmukh says is not heard." God Almighty listens to the gurumukh. "God Almighty hears whatever the perfect Master speaks, and that alone happens in this creation." Here we get confused! There are always people who oppose the Masters and torture them. So why don't Masters destroy those who bother them? If one curses someone who bothers him, he cannot be called patient. If one is poor and finds fault in God, he cannot be called content. We don't know what we should ask of God, so why would he listen to us? We ask for worldly things and we get them, but from them many problems are created, many difficulties arise, and then we suffer. That is why Farid Sahib says, "Make a bow of patience and let your patience be the bowstring. In this way when you shoot the arrow, God Almighty will not let it miss the target." Masters always pray

The Pain of Separation

to God, "O Lord, bless them with patience. Cool down their desires and have mercy on them."

> *Those who are patient abide in patience; in this way, they burn their bodies. They are close to the Lord, but they do not reveal their secret to anyone.*

Now he says, "What kind of life do such Mahatmas live?" They have an amazing kind of determination in their patience. They live their life according to the rules of nature. They never tell people, not even by mistake, that they have met with God, that they are the messenger of God or that they are the Lord or Prophet. No. He says that they live a very ordinary kind of life. "Those who are patient abide in patience; in this way, they burn their bodies." If they have pain in their body, they bear it. We can have patience only if we accept pain. "They are close to the Lord, but they do not reveal their secret to anyone."

There was a king in Rome and in his court he asked his ministers and everyone else present there, "What is patience and what is gratefulness?" Everyone answered according to their intellect, but the king was not satisfied. He sent one of his ministers to India, to the court of Aurangzeb, saying, "It is possible that you may get the answer there, as he has many scholars and learned people in his court. If he is not able to answer, over there is one fakir by the name of Sarmad; go and meet him as well." So, the minister went to Aurangzeb and said, "My Lord has sent me here and I would like to ask, 'What is patience and what is gratefulness?'" All the scholars were present there, but neither Aurangzeb nor his scholars could satisfactorily answer the question.

The minister then came out of the court and asked the people, "Is there any fakir by the name of Sarmad here?" Someone told him, "Yes, there is, but he is imprisoned by Aurangzeb. Aurangzeb the king opposes sadhus and fakirs and asks them to perform miracles.

Real sadhus and fakirs do not perform miracles. They believe that to bear all pain in the will of God is the biggest miracle. Sarmad is under heavy imprisonment, heavily locked up. Furthermore, they whip him and do not give him enough food to eat. They give him just one chapati of millet, one small lump of salt and a cup of water."

Let Patience Become Your Nature

Somehow that minister from Rome got inside the prison and called for Sarmad. It was dark in there. Sarmad didn't have any clothes on his body. He came near the bars and asked, "Who is calling me?" As soon as Sarmad said that, the guard, a demonic looking person who used to whip him, came and whipped him. Sarmad didn't even sigh. Quietly he bore that. Soon they brought his food which he ate after offering it to God Almighty and thanking him for it. The minister told Sarmad, "I have come to ask you this question; what is patience and what is gratefulness? Please tell me." Sarmad said, "I have already given you the answer, but you didn't understand. Come back tomorrow and bring a sheet and a pitcher of water and I will show you." The minister said, "But there are locks everywhere." Sarmad replied, "Don't worry. Lord Almighty, who has brought you here from Rome, will bring you here again." The next day he came and nature helped and unlocked the doors. Sarmad washed himself with the water the minister had brought and wiped off his body. He then said, "Sit here with me in meditation. Don't say anything and get up only when I ask you to." What did the minister see within, in the inner planes? He saw that many great powers, who were functioning within in those planes, were requesting Sarmad to allow them to destroy the kingdom of Aurangzeb. However, Sarmad was keeping quiet, saying, "It is the will of God." The minister was astonished to see how powerful Sarmad was and how those people had not recognized his power. He was astonished, looking at Sarmad, to see that he owned so many powers and still was not using them despite the great pain he was enduring on his body.

In the same way, there was a time when Master Kirpal was repeatedly asking Baba Sawan Singh, "You yourself do the remaining work of Naam initiation. You can cure your sickness. Please do it. We cannot bear seeing you like this." One day, in the divine will, Baba Sawan Singh Ji asked Master Kirpal to come and sit beside him. Baba Sawan Singh was lying on his bed and he said, "Today the decision is going to be made in Sach Khand." He gave his attention to Master Kirpal, and Master Kirpal saw in Sach Khand many Saints; Kabir Sahib, Guru Nanak, Maulana Rumi, Shams-i-Tabriz and all the Saints were sitting there. All the perfect Masters who had reached Sach Khand agreed on keeping Baba Sawan Singh Ji in

The Pain of Separation

this world for a little longer. However, Baba Jaimal Singh Ji did not accept that. He said, "The conditions are very bad at present; I won't let him be there any longer." In all times, devotees who have the desire to know reality are given such experiences, but we should look within and see with what thought and desire we sit in meditation. It won't work if we have one thing in our heart and make the effort for something else. You cannot deceive him who resides within you. So, this is how that minister got the answer to his question about what is patience and gratefulness and how the devotees of God remain in patience and gratefulness.

In the same way, when Mansur was hanged his hands were going to be chopped off. The executioners said that they had orders to cut off his hands. He said, "You may do so. I don't need these hands because I have spiritual hands and I can reach the heavens by clinging to the minarets of heaven with those hands." Then they said that they had orders to cut off his feet. He said, "Go ahead. I don't need them as I have spiritual feet by which I can reach Sach Khand." Then they said that they had to take out his eyes. He said, "Take them out as I don't need them either. I have those spiritual eyes which see my beloved Lord." After cutting off all those things, when they said that they had to cut off his tongue, he said, "Wait a minute. Let me express my gratitude to my beloved Lord with this tongue." He said, "O Lord, it was not within my power to pass this test. It is only through your grace that I have not failed you." When God Almighty asked Mansur if he would like them to be punished, he replied, "If you want me to say something, I would pray, please forgive them, so that they may know what Mansur has for them in his heart." Saints have an amazing amount of patience in them.

Guru Arjan Dev underwent inhuman tortures. He was made to sit on a heated pan, with fire burning underneath it. He was put in boiling water. Still his torturers were not content; they threw hot sand on his head. Mian Mir, who was his friend, went to see him and said, "What is this! Just give me an order and I can raze the city of Lahore to the ground." Guru Arjan Dev said, "Mian Mir, even I can do this but who would obey the will of the Master?" "Sweet is thy will O Lord, Nanak begs for the riches of Naam." The daughter-in-law of Chandu Sawai, the man by whose orders Guru

Let Patience Become Your Nature

Arjan Dev Ji was being tortured, came to know about what was happening and she set out to see Guru Arjan Dev. You know if your Master is being tortured, what would you not do to save him and have his darshan? When she was going to see him, she was stopped by the guards and she gave up all her ornaments and jewelry to them, just so she could go and have his darshan. A historian poet described that moment, saying, "Today, catastrophe has fallen on Lahore; the beautiful life is suffering pains. Guru Arjan is sitting on a heated pan and hot sand is being poured on his head. My life is collapsing within, who could support it?"

> *O man, if you let patience become your nature and implant it within your being,*
> *You will grow into a great river; you will not break off into a tiny stream.*

Now he says to make your patience so strong and determined that it stays with you at all times. Don't become like a river which overflows its banks and destroys whatever comes in its way. Don't give up patience and curse others. Don't perform miracles. He says if you do all that, what is the use of being patient in the beginning? Mahatma Chattar Das had said, "Chattar Das says, my prestige remains if my relationship with you is maintained till the end, O Lord." Many ups and downs come in our life. If a person remains firm in those times, he will survive.

Masters tell us a story of a Sadhu who used to pass by a prostitute's house every day, and she would ask him, "Is this your beard or a bush?" He would keep quiet. However, when his end time came, he called her and said, "Daughter, ask that question today." She said, "I asked it every day and you didn't reply." He replied, "How can you trust the mind? That scoundrel would have made me fall. Dear daughter, today I am carrying my beard unstained. I am saying this to you while I am in the grave." Farid Sahib also says the same thing.

There is an overwhelming story of Farid Sahib's life. He used to work as a *sevadar*[1] for his Master. He would bring water, heat it up and make a bath for

---

[1] One who does seva or service for the Master.

The Pain of Separation

his Master. In those days there was no convenient means to heat up water; people would burn firewood to do that. Since they did not have matchsticks to light the fire like they do today, they would keep the fire burning all the time. Once the fire at Farid Sahib's place went out and the only place with a fire burning nearby was at a prostitute's house. Farid Sahib saw that her servants had hookahs going. He had never gone to that place before because the prostitute would always try to seduce him, saying, "Everyone except you comes here. Why don't you also come?" He would always put his head down and take his attention to his Master. But on that day, since he didn't have any other way to get fire, he went there. She asked him, "Why have you come here? You never come." He said that he wanted the fire. She replied, "You have to pay the price for it." He asked, "What is the cost?" She said, "Your eye." Farid Sahib did not hesitate even for a second. He at once took out his eye and gave it to her. Seeing this the prostitute started trembling in fear. She said to herself, "I had only made a joke but he didn't get it and really took out his eye." She was terrified. Farid Sahib also didn't want his Master to know about this so he bandaged his eye and stopped the blood. He heated water for his Master and brought it to him. The Master saw the bandage and asked, "What is wrong with you? Why have you put a bandage on your eye this early in the morning?" He replied, "Master, the eye has come." In Punjabi language we say "the eye has come" when the eye is infected or if there is any illness of the eye. His Master said, "Son, if the eye has come, why have you covered it? Open the bandage." He just said it normally. When Farid Sahib removed the bandage, his eye was intact. This was not a miracle. He did not do that to cause harm to anyone. We people use these kinds of stories to assert that the past Masters performed miracles. Those Masters did not do such things to impress others or out of egoism. It happened naturally. Baba Sawan Singh Ji used to say nature itself takes care of the Masters' affairs. As it was said earlier, "God Almighty does not let their arrows miss the target." God doesn't let the words Masters speak go to waste.

> *O Farid, it is difficult to be a dervish, a holy Saint; it is easier to love when you get the buttered bread (riches).*
> *Only a rare few follow the way of the Saints.*

Let Patience Become Your Nature

Now he says it is very difficult to become a dervish. People do try to imitate them, but they "love buttered bread." When God Almighty gives us wealth, name and fame, etc., we say, "You see how gracious God is." But when we lose something, we find fault with him. So, Farid Sahib says it is very difficult to imitate the Saints. Our love for God exists only when we "get buttered bread." Bulleh Shah had said, "We sing all night where the pots and griddle rattle."

Shah Sarf was a wealthy man and his wife was also a devotee. Once he thought, "Let me see if Farid himself does the things he preaches." He and his wife then held a religious event and invited all the sadhus and fakirs of the area. They prepared good food for everyone else but for Farid Sahib the wife prepared a dish made out of twelve-year-old chickpeas, which were stale and had become bitter. She did not even put salt in that dish. Everyone was fed and everyone else ate happily. However, when Farid Sahib saw his food, it didn't look good. When he put a morsel in his mouth, it was bitter, so he didn't eat it. After a while, Shah Sarf came there and asked if everyone had eaten. They said, "Yes, we have all eaten except Farid Sahib. He is still sitting there." When Shah Sarf asked Farid Sahib why he was not eating, he replied. "It is without salt and is bitter. At least put some salt in it." Shah Sarf looked at his wife, who said, "I had made this food for the fakirs. I didn't know there were people here who craved tasty foods." At that time Farid Sahib said to himself, "Oh my mind! You love God for the buttered bread (riches), but pretend to be a dervish who accepts (things) as they are given."

My body is cooking like an oven; my bones are burning like firewood.
If my feet become tired, I will walk on my head, if I can meet my Beloved.

Do not heat up your body like an oven, and do not burn your bones like firewood.
What harm have your feet and head done to you? Behold your Beloved within yourself.

Now he lovingly says, "If I get tired walking on the path of God, I would walk on my head. If I have to make my body like an oven and burn my

The Pain of Separation

bones like firewood, I am ready to do it if I can only meet God Almighty by doing that." But Guru Nanak Dev Ji Maharaj says, "Look here, O Dear One, what is the use of burning your bones? What is the use of walking on your head? What is the need to suffer so many hardships? God Almighty, whom you want to realize, is not out there in the forests, he is not on the mountains; he is sitting within you. Why do you give so much pain to your body?"

> *I search for my Beloved, but my Beloved is already with me.*
> *O Nanak, the unseen Lord cannot be seen; he is revealed only to the gurumukh.*

Now Guru Nanak Sahib says, "I was searching for my Beloved in the best temples, in the best communities and religions and in the best rites and rituals, but I didn't know that my Beloved lives with me all the time, whether I am awake or asleep. He walks with me when I walk." When we go to the Masters, they connect us with God Almighty, who is calling us in the form of Shabd Dhun, the Sound Current, and make us have the darshan of the light within. It may only be a little according to our karmas, but we do get some capital. This is the gurumukhs' property. God Almighty is manifested within them in the form of light and sound. If you were to go to them, you don't need to suffer outer pain. They will tell you how he is residing within you.

> *Seeing the swans swimming, the cranes became excited.*
> *The poor cranes were drowned to death, with their heads below the water and their feet sticking out above.*

Swans can swim a long distance whereas cranes can only swim a short distance. He says that a crane imitated a swan but it drowned. His head went below the water and his feet came above the water. In the same way, looking at a Beloved of God doing devotion, it came in the mind of a hypocrite sadhu that he should also become like him. The hypocrite sadhu was impressed by the number of people following the true devotee. He

Let Patience Become Your Nature

started wearing the same kind of clothes as the true Beloved of God, learned to act and pose like him. But when he came to cross the ocean in the region of Kal, where even the greatest ones fear to go, the agents of Kal tied him up and hung him upside down. The interview which Sunder Das had with Master Kirpal is known to many people as it happened in front of many people. You know that Master Kirpal asked Sunder Das to close his eyes and see how many hypocrites there were and how they were being punished. Sunder Das gave out the number of hypocrites and described their punishments. Mastana Ji used to say that a hypocrite thinks that by touching something he will turn it into parshad but there is no sin more severe than deceiving someone's soul. The effect of such a sin is not erased even in seven lifetimes.

I thought he was a great swan, so I associated with him.
If I had known that he was only a wretched crane, I would never in my life have touched him.

In Goindwal, a hypocrite sadhu came to Guru Amar Dev Ji Maharaj. Guru Amar Dev Ji gave him a lot of respect and made him sit close to himself. He would even let him sit on the same dais with him while doing satsang. Guru Sahib had one rosary, with very precious beads in it. That hypocrite sadhu would always look at it and plan to steal it. One day Guru Sahib left his rosary on the dais and went away. Right then that sadhu took the rosary and hid it under the sheet covering the cushion he was sitting on. When Guru Sahib returned, the rosary was missing. Everyone looked for it but could not find it. Suddenly the wind blew off the sheet under which the rosary was hidden. One of the dear ones snatched it away from the hypocrite sadhu and said, "Here is the rosary!" So, Farid Sahib says, "I thought he was a great swan, so I associated with him. If I had known that he was only a wretched crane, I would never in my life have touched him." Guru Arjan said, "I understood him as a sadhu and that is why I made him sit with myself. Had I known that he was a crane, who only closes his eyes to show off that he is a devotee, there was no way that I would have allowed him to sit with me."

The Pain of Separation

In the same way, a person wearing saffron-colored clothes came to the *dera*[2] of Baba Sawan Singh Ji and asked for some seva to do. He asked for the seva of ringing the bell at three a.m. to wake up the dear ones. Baba Sawan Singh gave him that seva. He did that job properly and maintained love and cordial relations with everyone there. However, one day he took three hundred rupees from a chief of the village and ran away. Why would he need to stay and ring the bell when he had gotten the money? Baba Sawan Singh used to laugh and say, "He rang the bell of three hundred rupees."

Similarly, in the ashram of Baba Bishan Das, there was a so-called sadhu who wore colored robes; I had seen him myself. He would keep his eyes closed most of the time and open them only occasionally. Baba Bishan Das warned everyone that he was a hypocrite and one day he would steal their money. There were many sadhus there at the ashram, some with initiation into the first Word and some with initiation into Two Words. They all were very impressed by that so-called sadhu, as he would always keep his eyes closed as if he was meditating all the time. They said, "How is it possible that such a sadhu would steal money? Baba Bishan Das is just speaking in general terms." Like here at 16 PS, at Baba Bishan Das' ashram there were two courtyards. People used to stay in the bigger courtyard and eat in the smaller one. One evening at dinner time everyone went to the smaller courtyard for dinner. That sadhu said, "I don't feel like going for dinner as my attention is attached within. All of you go and let me sit." Even at that time Baba Bishan Das warned them saying, "You have left him alone over there. He must be going through your pockets." But who would listen? Before they came back after having dinner, he had collected all the money from their belongings; some had two rupees, some had three and so forth, and he ran away. When the other sadhus came back, they saw that their books, their clothes, their pillow covers, everything was all ripped up and their money was gone. There was a very strong sevadar at the ashram named Gurdayal Singh. He set off with his iron-bound bamboo stick

---

[2] Colony, sometimes used as another term for ashram or retreat center.

Let Patience Become Your Nature

to catch that sadhu, thinking that he must have not gotten too far away. However, Baba Bishan Das Ji said, "For how long have I been warning you? Now I will compensate you for your loss. Let him go. He got what he wished for." That is why Guru Amar Dev Ji Maharaj says, "I understood him as a swan (a true devotee). If I had known that he was a fake sadhu like a crane, who pretends to be meditating, why would I have given him a place next to me?"

> *Who is a swan, and who is a crane, if God blesses him with his glance of grace?*
> *If it pleases him, O Nanak, he changes a crow into a swan.*

Now Guru Amar Dev Ji Maharaj says, "You see, dear ones, in the eyes of God Almighty there is no crane or swan. He lovingly nourishes everyone and supports them equally." It is not difficult for him to make a swan out of a crane; he can even make a crow into a swan. The thing which is required is that we should desire to become a swan. What is the food of a crow? Dirt. When do we have the qualities of a crow? When we indulge in pleasures. However, when meditators get a taste of Shabd Naam, they discard all indulgences and, just like that, they become a swan.

> *There is only one bird in the lake, but there are fifty trappers.*
> *This body is caught in the waves of desire. O my True Lord, you are my only hope!*

Now he says, "Look here, O Dear Ones, there is only one jiva and to trap him there are five forces. There are five senses and five acting organs of senses, mind, intellect and other forces, which total fifty. They all trap one jiva." If one is not trapped in doing bad deeds, they trap him in good deeds. Lord Krishna said, "Neither good karmas nor bad karmas can save the soul from the clutches of Kal." Good deeds bind us like golden chains and bad deeds are like iron chains. At present, we may be sweeping the streets, but by doing good deeds we may come back as a king and take our bed from the streets to the palace. The broom goes out of our hand

The Pain of Separation

and the reins for ruling the kingdom come into them. Masters do not say that we will not get anything for our good deeds. They say, "No, brothers, whatever karmas you do, you will have to pay them off." That is why here he says, "This body is caught in waves of desire." One gets caught in those waves of desires and does not want to come out. Shabd Naam, the Master and the Almighty Lord are the only ones who can take him out, but he doesn't listen to them.

> *What is that word, what is that virtue, and what is that magic mantra?*
> *What are those clothes which I can wear to captivate my Husband Lord?*

Some seeker soul asked a question, "Farid Ji, what is that word, what is that mantra, repeating which I can control my Husband Lord? What clothes should I wear by which the Husband Lord can be controlled? Please teach me that." Farid answers in the following lines.

> *Humility is the word, forgiveness is the virtue, and sweet speech is the magic mantra.*
> *Wear these three robes, O Sister, and you will captivate your Husband Lord.*

Be humble, adopt forgiveness and repeat the mantra that the Sant Satguru have given to you all the time, whether you are awake or asleep. These are the only clothes that, if you wear them, O Dear Sister, the Husband Lord will come under your control. He will do what you will ask him to do.

> *Even if you are wise, be ignorant;*
> *Even if you are powerful, be weak;*
> *Share with others, even if there is nothing to share.*
> *Rare is one who is known as such a devotee.*

He says, "Who becomes successful in this path?" One has to be like a forty-day-old child even if he has all knowledge and wisdom. Don't let your intellect poke its nose into things. How can God Almighty be present where you allow your intellect to poke its nose? "Even if you are powerful,

Let Patience Become Your Nature

be weak." Sarmad had all the powers; what was it that he could not do? But no, he accepted the will of the Lord. Guru Gobind Singh Ji's father was martyred, his house was plundered, his children were buried in the walls, but still he didn't curse anyone in a fit of rage. When his four sons were all martyred, people felt a lot of pain but he said, "No, today I am at peace. Today I have returned the gift of sons which God Almighty had given to me and now I am totally free." We all may say such words but it is very difficult to do it. But he who does it becomes perfect. So, he says, "Even if you are wise, be ignorant; even if you are powerful, be weak." If one can do anything but still does not do it because it is not in the will of God, only he can be called a devotee.

Do not utter even a single harsh word; your True Lord and Master abides in all.

Do not say a bad word to anyone because that true Husband Lord is sitting within everyone. If we are saying bad words to anyone and are hurting anyone, we, in fact, are hurting God Almighty and are saying bad words to him.

Do not break anyone's heart; these are all priceless jewels.

He says, "Do not injure anyone's heart, as all hearts are like precious jewels. All souls are like precious jewels; they are holy and pure." Before saying anything to anyone, just consider what effect our words will have on him.

The minds of all are like precious jewels; to harm them is not good at all.
If you desire your Beloved, then do not break anyone's heart.

If you are fond of, yearn for and desire meeting God Almighty, try not to hurt anyone's heart. Hurting anyone's heart is the biggest sin.

Sometimes the Negative Power makes sevadars fight with each other. Once, two of Baba Sawan Singh Ji's sevadars fought with each other. Baba Sawan Singh Ji ignored them while he walked past them. They followed

The Pain of Separation

him, so he stopped and asked them what the matter was. One said, "I hit him because he abused me." Baba Ji said, "Look here, O Dear One, where did his abusive words hurt you? It is not visible but the blow you gave him has injured him; the blood is visible. If you had not paid attention to his abusive words, they would have passed like the passing wind and would have not hurt you. Now what punishment can I give to you both as both of you acted the same? He spoke bad words and you hurt him. If you had ignored the words and not hit him, it would have been better."

In these shlokas Farid Sahib very lovingly explained to us how we should remain in the will of God. He explained how our life should be and how we should adopt patience and contentment at all times in all our life. He has given us encouragement to live our life in the way it should be lived. It is our duty to make our lives successful and remain in the will of God Almighty.

Chapter 8

The Alms of Devotion and Love

This year I have done a lot of satsangs on the bani of Sheikh Farid and today also I am going to comment on his bani. Sheikh Farid was born in a Muslim family. He came in contact with Sufi Mahatmas. Sufi means purehearted one, one whose within is where only Naam prevails, and nothing of the world exists. One with such a heart is called a Sufi.

The life of Sheikh Farid is very similar to my own life as far as performing austerities and things like that are concerned. I would say that he performed more austerities, that he renounced a lot more, than I did.

Our Satguru, Baba Sawan Singh Ji, used to say that if anyone searches for God Almighty sincerely, if anyone searches for something sincerely, he definitely becomes successful in that, because God Almighty always responds to prayers which we do sincerely. He also used to say that if in our sincere search for God Almighty we leave the body without completing that search, without realizing God Almighty, even then whatever we have done in our search for him is not wasted. We get a better human body in the next lifetime in which we meet the perfect Master. In that way, he used to say that the search which we do sincerely for God Almighty is not less than devotion to God.

Farid Sahib suffered a lot of hunger and thirst even though he was born in a very noble family. He was married to the daughter of the ruler of Delhi at that time. But love is after all love; yearning is after all yearning.

The Pain of Separation

When real love and yearning are created within someone that person throws away power, throws away the throne and starts doing the devotion of God.

You know that all of us are born in one or another religion prevailing in this world, and devotees of God cannot get along with worldly people. Those worldly people are always attached to the rites and rituals of the religion in which they were born, whereas the devotees of God have faith in God Almighty himself. That is why there is always conflict between devotees of God and worldly people.

Sheikh Farid was opposed when he did not do things according to the rites and rituals of the Muslim religion; there was a conflict between him and the religious people. In those days the work of doing justice was in the hands of the kazis, and the work of giving education was in the hands of the maulvis.

When Sheikh Farid was asked, "Why don't you offer prayers and why don't you do the fast?" he replied, "Look here, O Dear Ones, to earn your livelihood with honest means is the real fasting and to have pity on all the souls, to see God Almighty in everyone, and to work hard in realizing God is the real prayer."

An incident happened during Sheikh Farid's life which he himself witnessed. There was a kazi who used to do justice for the people in a village, and it so happened that in that village there was one poor weaver who used to own a piece of land, but by force one farmer had taken over that land. Now it was in the hands of the kazi to see that justice was done, so that is why that poor weaver went to him and, giving him a very beautiful turban, told him his story. He told him, "Kazi Ji, I am a very poor person. I have my children to look after. You know what the reality is, what the facts are; that land is owned by me, but that farmer has taken it over by force. When you sit for making a decision, kindly find in my favor. I am offering this beautiful turban to you." The kazi took that turban and wore it on his head, and the weaver was very happy.

The farmer, the landlord, was stronger and richer than the poor weaver. He took one very nice cow and he left that cow with the kazi. That cow used to give a lot of milk. The kazi was also very pleased with the landlord,

The Alms of Devotion and Love

because now he could drink milk every morning and every evening, and his son also used to like that milk a lot. So, he was more pleased with the landlord.

When the day came that he had to give judgment, the kazi started to decide in favor of the landlord, but the poor weaver said, "Kazi Ji, at least look at my turban." The kazi replied, "O Fool, your turban has been eaten up by that cow."

Farid Sahib said that this is not real justice. To have pity on all souls and to treat them fairly is real justice, and that is real prayer. If you are sincere, if you are true, only then can you offer real prayers to Almighty God.

Something similar also happened in the life of Kabir Sahib. He said that it is a pity that those people who have the power of doing justice do not give it in favor of the poor people and they always favor the rich people. He said, "Whatever the kazis and mullahs have written, I have left everything of that behind and I am doing the devotion of God."

Farid Sahib had real love, yearning and devotion for his Master. He had a lot of faith in his Master. He had caught hold of Sant Mat very firmly. It was not like he had one thing in his heart and something different in his mouth. Whatever he had in his heart, only that came out from his mouth.

There is another incident connected to the life of Sheikh Farid. Sheikh Farid spent a lot of time with his Master, serving him and taking care of him. In the place where he used to live with his Master, there was a house of a prostitute not far from their house, and that prostitute always tried to trap Sheikh Farid. But since Sheikh Farid was devoted to Almighty God, he never paid any attention to that prostitute. You know that whenever we start doing the devotion of God, the Negative Power always creates traps so that we stop doing the devotion of God. The devotees do not get trapped because they know what their goal is and they go on working towards their goal. So, Sheikh Farid never paid any attention to that prostitute, no matter what she said or what she did to him. He would always look down and just walk by that house and not pay any attention to her remarks.

In those days there was nothing like matches, so people used to preserve fire in their homes. Sometimes that fire would go out and it would become very difficult for people to light the firewood. They would have

The Pain of Separation

to go to somebody else's home to borrow the fire. Once it so happened that the fire in the home of Sheikh Farid went out at a time when he had to heat up some water for his Master to take a shower. Since he did not have any fire in his home he went to that prostitute. Before that he had never been to that prostitute's home and he had never talked with her, so when he went there to ask for the fire, she was surprised. She thought, "Up until now this person has never come to me and he has never responded to the remarks I have made about him. Today it is very good that he has come to me by himself and today is my chance." So, when Sheikh Farid asked her for some fire, she said that the price of the fire is an eye.

Sheikh Farid did not wait even for a moment to think. He at once took out his eye and placed it in front of the prostitute. When the prostitute saw that he had taken out his eye she became very nervous. She realized that she had made a mistake, because he was a devotee of God and she should not have said that. After that he took the fire from the prostitute's home and, tying a bandage on his eye, he warmed up some water and he went to his Master. When he came in front of the Master, his Master saw the bandage and he asked Sheikh Farid what was wrong with his eye.

In Punjabi there is a saying whenever anyone has some infection or pain in his eye; they say, "The eye has come." So, like that, when Sheikh Farid's Master asked him what was wrong with his eye, he said, "Master, my eye has come." His Master replied, "Dear one, when the eye has come why do we have to put a bandage on it? Remove the bandage." When he removed the bandage both his eyes were intact. This was the devotion of Sheikh Farid. He did not have shaky faith in the Master; he had complete faith in the Master and whatever his Master told him to do he did that.

This is something which we all should pay attention to. We should think about this patiently. Saints always say that we should spare ourselves from the tricks of the mind, because mind is such a thing that he will always lay such traps and he will trap you in those traps. That is why they always say that we should be aware of the tricks of the mind and we should always protect ourselves from the traps of the mind. All of us satsangis should think about this; just imagine, if we are placed in the same situation,

The Alms of Devotion and Love

if we have to face that situation, will we remain devoted like Sheikh Farid? Can we do any sacrifice like this for our Master?

Those who have true love for the Lord in their heart are the only true ones.
Those who have one thing in their heart and something else in their mouth are the untrue ones.

Farid Sahib lovingly explains to us who are the true ones in the court of the Master, who are the sincere ones in the court of the Lord. Only those who have real love in their heart for the Master are the true ones. Master used to say that heart talks to heart. That is why those who have real, sincere love in their heart and real devotion on their face are accepted in the court of the Lord. Farid Sahib says that those who have the same thing in their heart and on their face are the perfect ones, and they are accepted and honored in the court of the Lord. But those who have one thing in their heart and something else on their face are not yet perfect ones, and they are not accepted in the court of the Lord.

It has not been a very long time since paper currency started being used. When I was very young, I remember having silver coins and coins of other metals as currency. Guru Nanak Sahib has also mentioned silver coins in his writings. In those days whenever anyone had to make any payment to the government, they would take coins to the treasurer. The treasurer would test those coins; he would accept the real ones and would throw out the unreal ones.

In the same way, Guru Nanak Sahib says that God Almighty accepts the true coins. He does not accept the false ones; he sends them into the cycle of illusion. After every death we are presented to Almighty God, and if we are true in his devotion, if we have done the devotion of Almighty God sincerely, then he accepts us and he allows us to go to his real home, Sach Khand. If we have not been true to his devotion, if we have not done the devotion sincerely, then he sends us into the cycle of eighty-four lakhs again.

Guru Nanak Sahib also says that when false jewelry is presented to a real goldsmith, its impurity is easily discovered. In the same way, when

The Pain of Separation

any false or imperfect master comes in front of a perfect disciple then his imperfection is easily discovered and he cannot face that disciple.

In the same way, if there is a perfect Master and if we are not yet perfect disciples, whenever we go to such a perfect Master, we will not be able to look into his eyes. We will not be able to face him, because our sins, our impurities, will not allow us, will not give us the courage to look into the eyes of the Master. That is why Masters always say that those so-called masters who give very good lectures outside in the world but who have different things in their heart than what they say from their mouth, they will not be able to face the perfect disciples, just as imperfect disciples cannot face the perfect Master.

That is why Masters always say that before going to any master and before taking refuge at the feet of any master, we should first find out about his way of living. You should find out whether he has done any meditation in his life, whether he has sacrificed twenty or thirty years of his life to do the devotion of God, and whether he is still doing meditation or not. That is why Masters always say that before taking anyone as a Master, first of all you should find out what his previous life has been like and how he is living his life now.

I do not mean to criticize anyone or comment upon anyone. But I would like to tell you why nowadays Gurudom has become the target of everyone's hatred, why people do not believe in this. You know that if anyone has been bitten by a snake, he will fear even a rope. In the same way, those who have been betrayed by a false master are afraid even to come near the perfect or true Masters. Truth never vanishes. Truth is never completely destroyed in this world. There is always some True Being in this world. People are involved in the mind and the sense-organs, but unless we rise above the level of the mind and the sense-organs, we can never become successful in finding out what is the truth.

You know that our beloved Master Kirpal was very learned. He was a great writer and a scholar. But he never said that a criterion of a perfect Master is that he is a good writer or a learned man. He always said, "It is not true that only a good writer or only a learned person can become a perfect Master." Master Sawan Singh Ji also said the same thing. He used to

The Alms of Devotion and Love

say, "If a Mahatma lives according to what he preaches, and if a Mahatma speaks exactly the same words which he has in his heart, such a Mahatma gets liberation for himself and he also liberates those who follow him."

In the beginning when I went to Delhi, many initiates of Master Kirpal came to see me. Many longtime initiates of Master Kirpal came to see me, and they all quoted from so many different books. Someone said this is written in this book, others said that is written in that book. Nobody told me anything more than that. I had only one response to all of them, and even now I have the same response to all of them. I say, "Dear ones, if you reach that place from where all these books have come out, the place in our within from where we think and where we have our intellect, then you do not need to quote from all these books. If you have seen that place with your own eyes then you do not need to quote from the books, you do not need to do anything, because when you go within then everything becomes clear to you. Everything there is very true, and you can see it with your own eyes."

Once Emperor Akbar asked Birbal, "What is the difference between the true and the false?" Birbal replied, "That is exactly like the difference between the eyes and the ears. With the ears you hear things and you know that it is not always possible to believe what you hear, but you do not have any difficulty believing in the things which you have seen with your own eyes." That is why I have always told the dear ones that you should go within and see things with your own eyes. Then you will not have to worry about believing the things that you are hearing.

Those who are imbued with love for the Lord are delighted by his vision.

Now he says that those who have become absorbed in Almighty God, in that real Shabd Naam, for them the darshan of Almighty God is their food and water. He says that only those whose everything is Almighty God are the real lovers of Almighty God. Kabir Sahib says, "O My Beloved, if you come in my sight, I will close my eyes so that I may not look at anyone else. I will capture you in my eyes so that I may not allow you to look at anyone else." Such a dear one who has a real love, a real devotion for Almighty

The Pain of Separation

God, sees his beloved Lord within everyone. Such a dear one, such a devotee of God, has real love for him.

Dear ones, have you not read that when Christ was being crucified God Almighty asked him, "What punishment should I give to these people?" Christ replied, "They are innocent people, they do not know. You should forgive them." Because he had such an eye that he saw only God Almighty within all of them, he said that they should be forgiven.

Those who forget the Naam are a burden on the earth.

Farid Sahib says, "Who does the earth feel as a burden? With whose sin does this earth tremble?" He says that only those who do not do the meditation of Shabd Naam, only those who do not believe in the existence of God Almighty, and only those who do bad deeds: their sins have become a burden on this earth. Kabir Sahib says, "Always fear those whom God Almighty has left out of doing his devotion." He says that those who have not been chosen by God Almighty for his devotion, those upon whom God Almighty has not showered his grace and those whom he has not brought to the path of his devotion, you should always be afraid of them, because they are not devoting themselves to God and in their egoism they are doing bad deeds.

Those whom God attaches to his feet are the true dervishes at his door (the doorkeepers of the divine court).

Farid Sahib says, "Who are the real dervishes, who are the real fakirs, and who are the real devotees? Only those whom God Almighty himself embraced, after coming to their homes."

Blessed are the mothers who gave birth to them; their coming to this world is successful.

Now he says that blessed was the father in whose home such a personality took birth and played as a child. Great was the mother who gave birth to

The Alms of Devotion and Love

such a child, and such a personality's coming into this world is also blessed and great.

You know how much we love and appreciate the mothers and fathers of the past Saints and Mahatmas, how the mother and father of Guru Nanak Dev Ji are appreciated. There are still many people who believe in them and who praise the parents of Guru Nanak Dev Ji Maharaj. Similarly, you know how respectfully we remember the parents of our beloved Master, Baba Sawan Singh, and how we glorify and praise the parents of our beloved Master Kirpal. We say that Hukam Singh was a blessed one, he was great, because in his home beloved Kirpal, who came only to shower grace on all souls, came into this world. We congratulate Gulab Devi also, because she was the one who gave birth to such a gem in this world.

In his bani Guru Nanak Dev Ji has written, "Blessed is the family in which the Master was born. Blessed is the mother who gave birth to such a child. Blessed is the Satguru who, after taking birth into this world, did not become dirty in the dirt of the world. Renouncing everything of this world, he did the devotion of God; he himself got liberation, and all those who came to him were also liberated. He received such a recognition from God Almighty that those who followed him were also liberated."

O God, you are the sustainer, endless, provider, limitless, and the unreachable one.

O God, you nourish everyone. You are unreachable; no one can reach you.

Those who recognize the truth I kiss their feet.

He says, "O God, you nourish everyone. You are unreachable, you are limitless. No one can reach you. You are unfathomable. If you give me the opportunity, I am ready to kiss the feet of those who have reached you and those who have realized you. If you shower grace on me, I will feel myself to be the most fortunate one. Give me the opportunity of kissing the feet of your Beloveds."

The Pain of Separation

O forgiving God, I seek your refuge.
Bless Sheikh Farid with the alms of devotion.

Now he says, "I have come to your refuge. Since you are the forgiving one, that is why I have come to your refuge, and I am asking only for the alms of devotion. I am stretching out my *jholi*,[1] and I am requesting you to fill up this empty bag of mine with the alms of your devotion and with your love."

---

[1] The front part of the loose shirts worn in India, which the devotees hold open as a means of accepting parshad. "Filling the jholi" thus becomes a term for giving grace.

The Alms of Devotion and Love

This ends Sant Ajaib Singh's comments on the verses of Sheik Farid. Below are the three additional verses of Farid's that were included in the Guru Granth.

Rag Asa, Shabd 2

Sheikh Farid says, "O dear one, attach yourself to God".
This body will become dust and will reside in the neglected graveyard.

You can meet the Lord today. O Sheikh Farid, if you control your bird-like desires which bother your mind.

Had I known that I was going to die and not return again,
I would have not ruined myself by getting attached to the unreal.

Speak the truth, live righteously, and do not speak falsehood.
The disciple should follow the path shown by the Master.

Seeing the youths crossing over, the hearts of the young soul-brides are encouraged.
Those who get attached to the gold are cut down with a saw.

O Sheikh, no one lived in this world forever.
The seat upon which we now sit, many others sat on it and have left.

As the kunjas (migratory cranes) appear in the month of Katik (October – November), forest fires in the month of Chet (March-April) and lightning in the month of Sawan (July-August),
And as the bride's arms adorn her husband's neck in winter,

Just like that, the traveler goes away; think about this in your mind.
It takes six months to form the body, but it breaks in a moment.

O Farid, the earth asks the sky, "Where have the ferrymen gone?"

The Pain of Separation

Some have been cremated, and some lie in their graves; their souls are suffering rebukes.

Rag Suhi, Shabds 1 & 2

Burning and burning, writhing in pain, I wring my hands.
I have gone insane, seeking my Husband Lord.
O my Husband Lord, you are angry with me in your mind.
The fault is with me, and not with my Husband Lord.

O my Lord and Master, I do not know your excellence and worth.
Having wasted my youth, now I come to regret and repent.

O black cuckoo, what qualities have made you black?
"I have been burnt by separation from my Beloved."
Without her Husband Lord, how can the soul-bride ever find peace?
When he becomes merciful, then God unites us with himself.

The lonely soul-bride suffers in the pit of the world.
She has no companions, and no friends.
Showering grace on me, God has united me with the company of the Sadhu (Master).
And when I look again, then I find God as my helper.

The path upon which I must walk is very depressing.
It is sharper than a two-edged sword, and very narrow.
That is where my path lies.
O Sheikh Farid, think of that path early on.

You were not able to make yourself a raft when you should have.
When the ocean is churning and over-flowing, then it is very difficult to cross over it.

Do not touch the safflower with your hands; its color will fade away, my dear.

The Alms of Devotion and Love

First, the bride herself is weak, and then, her Husband Lord's order is hard to bear.
Milk does not return to the breast; it will not be collected again.

Says Farid, O my companions, when our Husband Lord will call,
The swan (soul) will depart, sad at heart, and this body will become a heap of dust.

GLOSSARY

Amar Das: (1479-1574) Third Guru of the Sikhs.

Arjan: (1563-1606) Fifth Guru of the Sikhs, compiled the Guru Granth Sahib.

Asafetida: a resinous gum with a very pungent odor, used as a spice in Indian cooking or as a digestive aid.

Ashram: Spiritual or retreat center.

Astral: Subtle region, the plane of creation above the physical plane.

Baba: Reverential prefix added to the name of old or holy men.

Banis: Verses or songs of the Saints.

Bhai: Literally "brother"; also used to designate a priest of the Sikh temples.

Bhajan: Spiritual verses of hymns generally meant to be sung. Also refers to the meditation practice of listening to the Sound Current.

Brahm or Brahmand: Second inner spiritual plane, on top of the physical and astral planes; also known as the causal plane or Trikuti.

Chapati: Indian flat bread.

Dacoit: Thief, professional criminal.

The Pain of Separation

Darshan: Gracious glance from a spiritual figure.

Dervish: Member of Sufi religious order, who has taken vows of poverty and austerity.

Dev: Lord, also a suffix added to names of spiritual figures.

Dhun: Sound, another name for the inner Sound Current of Shabd.

Fakir: Muslim term for a renunciate or Saint.

Gobind Singh: (1660-1708) Tenth and final Guru of the Sikh religion.

Gurdwara: A Sikh place of worship.

Guru Granth Sahib: The central religious scripture of Sikhism, compiled by Guru Arjan Dev.

Gurumukh: Literally, "mouthpiece of the Guru", a highly advanced or perfect disciple. The opposite of a manmukh.

Jaggery: An unrefined form of sugar derived from sugar cane.

Jaimal Singh: (1838-1903) Master of Baba Sawan Singh.

Jaldhara: An austerity in which the person repeats a mantra while standing outside, usually in the cold winter months, and a slow flow of very cold water falls onto his head.

Ji: Suffix added to personal names as a mark of love and respect.

Jiva: Embodied or individual soul.

Glossary

Kabir: (1440-1518) A great Indian Saint and contemporary of Guru Nanak. The modern age of Sant Mat in which the practice of the inner Sound Current is openly taught began with Kabir. See also *The Ocean of Love: The Anurag Sagar of Kabir* for additional material on this profound spiritual figure.

Kal: The entity who is ruler of the three perishable worlds (physical, astral and causal) and responsible for their maintenance. Kal, also known as Dharam Rai (the Lord of Judgement) or the Lord of Death, is responsible for keeping the souls trapped within the perishable worlds, in contrast to the Positive Power, manifested in the Saints and responsible for liberating the souls.

Kazi: An Islamic legal scholar and judge.

Karma: The law of action and reaction which governs the fate of each person. Also used as a term for a given action which creates karma, or for fate, the result of previous actions. See also *Life and Death* by Kirpal Singh for an in-depth explanation.

Lakhs 84: Refers to the cycle of incarnations through the eighty-four hundred thousand species.

Langar: Free community kitchen sponsored by a religious group.

Maharaj: Literally, "great king"; used as a term of greatness or respect.

Mahatma: Literally, "great soul"; used to designate a holy person.

Manmukh: Literally, "mouthpiece of the mind", one who is under the control of the mind and is worldly minded. The opposite of a gurumukh, or one who is the mouthpiece of the Guru.

The Pain of Separation

Maya: Illusion, the feminine aspect of Kal, separates the soul from God. Also used as a term for the material things of this world.

Muni: Refers to a holy man, a sage, a devotee; also a religious person who has taken a vow of silence.

Naam: The Creative Power of God; his original expression, the essence of the whole manifested universe and each individual. Also called Word, Shabd, Kalma, etc. See also *Naam or Word* by Kirpal Singh for a detailed explanation of this key spiritual term.

Nanak: (1469-1539) First Guru of the Sikhs, honored by them as the founder of the Sikh religion. A younger contemporary of Kabir, he had close associations with Kabir and continued his mission, ignoring religious and caste differences and teaching the practice of the inner Sound Current.

Negative Power: Another term for Kal.

Pahar: A watch, the traditional unit of time in ancient India equal to three hours.

Parshad: Food blessed by a Saint, given as a way of bestowing grace.

Pathan: Brave tribal people of West Pakistan and Afghanistan.

Pathi: The person who sings or change the verses that serve as a basis for the Master's spiritual discourses.

Pir: A Sufi teacher or spiritual Master.

Puranas: Ancient Hindu scriptures.

Glossary

Ram Das: (1534-1581) Fourth Guru of the Sikhs.

Rishi: In Hinduism, an inspired poet or sage. Usually refers to sages of ancient times to whom the Vedas were revealed.

Sach Khand: The region of Truth, the fifth inner plane and the first purely spiritual one. Seat of the Supreme Lord, not subject to decay or dissolution, it is the goal that Saints set for their disciples as is not until this stage is attained that true liberation is achieved.

Sadhu: Popularly used in India to mean a wandering monk or renunciate; literally "a disciplined soul." Also used in Sant Mat to indicate one who has attained the third plane.

Sahib: An Indian term meaning "Master," used as a term of respect for a man in a position of authority.

Samadhi: Absorption in God. Deep meditation, a state of concentration in which all consciousness of the outer world is transcended.

Sangat: The spiritual congregation.

Sant Mat: The Path of the Masters. The essence of all religions, it is attached to none and consists of the practice of Surat Shabd Yoga.

Sat Lok: "Region of Truth"; used to denote the purely spiritual regions of Sach Khand and above.

Satguru: Literally, "True Guru"; a perfect Master, a fully realized soul who has been commissioned by God to teach the inner path to seekers after truth.

Satsang: A discourse given by a Saint or Master on the subject of spirituality. Also refers to the congregation where seekers gather to hear the teachings of the Saints.

Satsangi: A term used to refer to a disciple of a true Master, or any seeker after truth, literally "one who attends satsang."

Seva: Selfless service in a spiritual cause.

Sevadar: One who does seva or service for the Master.

Shabd: Another term for Naam or the inner Sound Current vibrating in all creation. Also used as a term for spiritual hymns.

Sheik: An official in a Muslim religious organization or order; a title added to the names of Muslim holy men out of respect by their followers.

Shloka: A Sanskrit term for a verse, hymn or poem using a specific meter; sometimes used to specify a verse or stanza of two lines.

Simran: Literally, remembrance. Used for remembrance of the Lord. Also repetition of a mantra such as that given by a true Master at the time of initiation.

Sound Current: Another term for Naam or Shabd, the audible life stream. Listening to the inner Sound Current is one of the meditation practices given at initiation by a perfect Master.

Sufi: Muslim mystic. The most advanced Sufis were perfect Masters.

Surat: Literally, "attention"; expression of the soul; Surat Shabd Yoga is the union of the attention with the Shabd or Word.

Swami Ji: (1818-1878) Shiv Dayal Singh of Agra, the Guru of Baba Jaimal Singh.

Glossary

Tapas: Austerities.

Teg Bahadur: (1621-1675) Ninth Guru of the Sikhs.

Trikuti: The second inner plane, the causal plane.

Vedas: The ancient sacred books of Hinduism; includes the Upanishads.

Word: Another term for Naam or Shabd. "In the beginning was the Word and the Word was with God and the Word was God." (John 1:1).

Words – Five Words and Two Words: The Five Words refers, on the outer level, to the mantra given by the Masters at initiation. They focus the soul's attention and function as passwords to the five planes. On the inner level, it refers to the manifestations of the inner Sound Current originating from the five different inner planes that the soul hears and merges with during its inward ascent. The Two Words refers to the first two of the Five Words given at initiation and provide passage through the first two planes but not beyond and refer to the manifestation of the inner Sound Current originating from the first two inner planes.

Other Titles Available from Sant Bani Ashram

by Sant Kirpal Singh Ji
The Way of the Saints
Baba Jaimal Singh
The Jap Ji
The Night Is A Jungle
The Light of Kirpal
God Power, Christ Power, Guru Power

by Sant Ajaib Singh Ji
Streams in the Desert
The Ocean of Love
The Two Ways
In the Palace of Love
The Rescue: The Vars of Bhai Gurdas
In Search of the Gracious One
The Ambrosial Hour: Collected talks of
Baba Sawan Singh, Kirpal Singh and Ajaib Singh

by other authors
Impact of a Saint, by Russell Perkins
Stumbling Toward God, by Russell Perkins
Rainbow on My Heart, by Kent Bicknell

For more information, a complete book list, to order books online or download PDFs of many of these books, please go to our website at:
santbaniashram.org
or email us at **sbapublications@gmail.com**

Made in United States
Troutdale, OR
10/14/2024